How to Build Your Own Tennis Court

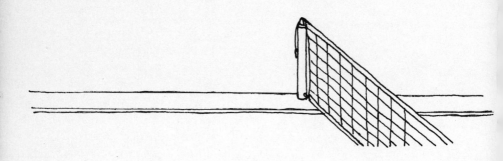

How to Build Your Own Tennis Court

ALAN ANDERSON

Illustrations by Ben Kuwata

A Sunrise Book • E. P. Dutton • New York

Library of Congress Cataloging in Publication Data
Anderson, Alan, 1917-
How to build your own tennis court.
"A Sunrise book."
Includes index.
1. Tennis courts—Design and construction. I. Title.
GV1002.A5   1977   624   77-6623
ISBN: 0-87690-251-4
Published simultaneously in Canada by Clarke,
Irwin & Company Limited, Toronto and Vancouver

10 9 8 7 6 5 4 3 2 1

First Edition

CONTENTS

ACKNOWLEDGMENTS

I wish to express my gratitude to:

Don Ackerson for having done it before me and for making it sound possible.

Robert M. Pirsig for his moving and edifying *Zen and the Art of Motorcycle Maintenance*.

John Fehsal for using his bulldozer with the deftness of a sculptor.

Ted Brubaker for laying down two hundred tons of rock like a pastry chef.

Tony Grando for being one of the most conscientious artisans I've ever known and his wife and sons for all their cheerful help.

Dick August for helping me put into words what you need to know about the transit.

My relatives and friends for raking and hauling and shoveling and mixing and raking some more—and for doing so many other things I have no room to mention.

And mostly my wife, Nancy, for not only giving me the courage to do it but working like a Trojan through it all—and for making sure ours was a *beautiful* tennis court, as well as a good one.

AUTHOR'S NOTE

My primary purpose in writing this book is to make it easier for you to build a tennis court with a minimum of professional assistance—and thus to eliminate a great deal of the cost.

The book is also aimed at

anyone who wants to have a court built and would like to be more knowledgeable about how it is done, so he or she can more intelligently choose a tennis-court contractor and will be better equipped to know what kind of job the contractor is doing.

anyone who wants to encourage the community or a small group of neighbors to build a court—or courts. Drawing on the talents of a number of people can make the job far simpler.

anyone who has a court and wants to repair it or have it repaired.

Prelude

How I became interested in
the subject myself and interested other
important people, like my wife.

It all started the day our next-door neighbors split up. He made
the obligatory move out of the house, and when she got tired of
being alone in the country with kids who treated the place as a
stopover between engagements, she put the house on the market.

And of course, the tennis court went with the house. *Our* tennis
court. Well, all right, *not* our tennis court. We had just come to
think of it as ours. After all, we had been playing on it for years—
whenever we wanted to.

The full import of the divorce and the sale didn't sink in right
away. A very nice family bought the house, and having bought it,
they proceeded to occupy it. Natural enough.

Then they began to use everything—the house, the pool, and
finally, the tennis court. Evidently, they took the view that having
bought the place, it was all theirs.

A great deal has been written about the responsibilities of a di-
vorcing couple for each other and for their children, if any. I can
find nothing in print on the profound obligations of such a couple
if they happen to own a tennis court and have tennis-playing
friends.

As the courtless days dragged by, we began to question our plight. Was our condition unalterable?

I went around talking to myself a lot about tennis courts and what they were and the meaning they had for mankind—which is to say, for me.

One day at the Tarrytown station, waiting for the 8:36, I suppose I must have been muttering again because a man next to me said, "I know a guy who built a tennis court *himself*."

Something must have told him that he couldn't stop there.

"Well, he got a few friends to help him, of course. Including me. Sort of a community venture. But Don figured it all out."

"Himself?" I asked.

"And a few friends," the man reminded me. "Of course, he's an engineer with Union Carbide. That probably made it easier for him."

"Who—what's his name?" My speech was fuzzy, blurred. "I'd like to ask him about it," I continued more firmly. I got the name and phone number.

Don Ackerson was indeed at Union Carbide, and he said he would be glad to talk about building a tennis court. He would also be glad to send me his United States Lawn Tennis Association (USLTA) * handbook on building tennis courts.

"There's a handbook?" I asked incredulously. Other people must have done it. It *wasn't* madness. "And you actually built a court?"

Yes, he had built a court—in fact, two courts. After completing the first one, a fast-dry court, he decided that it would be a good idea to have a nonporous court, which could be used through more seasons of the year. "I'll lend you the handbook if you like," he offered.

That did it. I began to believe what I had once thought of as fantasy.

The handbook arrived in the mail a few days later. I read it, talked to my wife about it, and walked around our place, pacing it off, looking at the position of the sun. And I talked to Don on

* Now USTA, having dropped the word *lawn* in 1975 because a grass surface has seldom been used in major competition in this country since the installation of crushed stone at the West Side Tennis Club, in Forest Hills.

the phone, filling in more details. Finally, my wife and I began to tell close friends. Watching their first reactions, we suffered some emotional setbacks, but we were well armed by then with fact and example—and were determined not to be wrong. After convincing some of our friends, our commitment deepened. We had already answered *why* and *where*. There was now no question of *whether*. There were only *how* and *when*.

I visited USLTA headquarters, which had recently moved to larger offices on Forty-second Street in New York City. Reflecting the meteoric growth of interest in the game since Don Ackerson had bought his manual for twenty-five cents, the one I bought was three dollars. By the time I started putting down this information for the world, the handbook price had climbed to five dollars. And while it proved an invaluable guide, it presupposes that you will use professional contractors for most of the work. Therefore we found that we had to proceed step by step, learning as we went.

What I have tried to do in this book is to give you the answers to all the questions we faced. You don't need to read the chapters in order if you are curious about information to be found three chapters ahead. However, once you start the actual work, I think you will find that it follows logically in the order of the book except when I have suggested otherwise.

I will start off with a few basic questions which must be answered before you even decide to build a court. Your answers will tell you whether to toss this volume into the attic, give it to a local charity, or plunge ahead.

1.

Why?

Those who have an inordinate, compulsive, overwhelming desire to play a lot of tennis today, tomorrow, and for the rest of their lives have experienced over and over again, in one form or another, the unbelievable emptiness of having *no place to play.*

There are long waiting lists of people who want to join tennis clubs across the country.

There are people waiting to play at every tennis court within a day's drive of their homes—and that's about the farthest even the addicted will go for a couple of sets.

When you arrive at the high school or tennis club or public park, you can see from afar that there is an empty court. By the time you pull into the parking lot, one of a number of things happens: a car cuts you off in the parking lot and four oafish chaps bolt onto the court while you are getting your gear out of the car, two eight-year-olds separate themselves from the drinking fountain where they've been hiding and dash back to pick up their game at two-all, or there is a small sign explaining that the court is reserved for lessons, which begin in precisely seven minutes. These are just examples.

There are people waiting to play at every tennis court within a day's drive.

Those who have had tennis courts in their lives upon which they could depend for their use almost at will have known the ultimate luxury for the tennis fanatic. Let us imagine a warm Saturday that dawns sunny and dry. You yawn, stretch, walk to the window to look out on the world, and there it is—an empty tennis court, with the net up, the lines down, and no one waiting.

"Hey," you call to your spouse, "guess what? Someone's left an empty tennis court in our front yard!"

My wife and I have been enjoying that miracle for several years now, and it is no less miraculous today than it was the first morning. Whenever I catch myself becoming used to the idea of having a court, I remind myself of all those moments of utter frustration and once again, I get a pleasurable chill.

Why do you want a tennis court?

Is there a tennis player who doesn't?

And because you want a tennis court, if you have room for one on your property, can you imagine anything else you could do that would benefit you, your family, your friends, and a whole tennis-loving nation as much as building one?

Next question . . .

Several questions remain to be answered positively before you

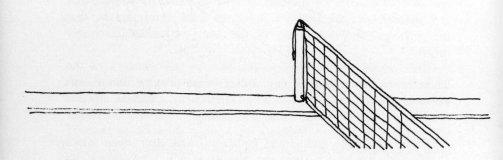

"Guess what? Someone's left an empty tennis court in our front yard!"

are ready to decide to do *it*. The big one, of course, is *how,* which is the essence of these pages. But I will postpone *how* until you have answered *where* because if you cannot answer that one, there is no point in going on.

The Next Question: Where?

The court area itself is only 78 feet by 36 feet. The playing area around this should ideally be 21 feet at each end and 12 feet at each side. These are USTA recommendations. If need be, the playing area outside the lines can be reduced by as much as 5 feet at each end and on each side, but this should only be considered if you cannot find an area 120 feet by 60 feet.

An additional requirement is that the length of the court be positioned approximately along the north-south axis. A tennis court that lies in a generally east-west direction will succeed in making all the players unhappy all the time the sun is shining.

And although we know you cannot make all the players happy all the time, you would do better to try to make all of the players happy *some* of the time.

If you don't have enough room to build on your own land, you might consider sharing the court with neighbors by purchasing land jointly and making an agreement for common ownership and responsibility. A court that is shared by four to six families provides ample playing time, a good supply of players, and of course, a happy division of cost and labor. I suggest that any sharing take the form of a written legal agreement so that the privileges and obligations of the joint ownership be clearly defined.

Other considerations concern the natural conformation of the land, the existence of rock and other immovable or almost immovable features. It isn't difficult to blast away a certain amount of rock, and it is simple to move a great deal of earth. But moving a great deal of rock or building on a steep slope or in swampy land—these must all be considered critical problems.

An additional factor that affects the enjoyment of the game is wind. If there is a way to afford yourself some shelter from trees or hills or other natural windbreaks, you should try to do so. But this is not crucial because barriers can be created by planting or by the use of canvas or even vines growing on the fence around the court. These matters are dealt with in detail in Chapter 10,

"How about here?"

pages 131–138. At this point our only purpose is to be sure that the project is *possible,* not to describe how to accomplish it.

It is also essential that you check out the local statutes—zoning laws, building codes, laws concerning the necessary distance from your property lines, the allowable height for a fence near a property line, and so forth—and perhaps seek the approval of your neighbors for a tennis court under their bedroom windows. It is surprising how many people object to something if it is a surprise and how much more cooperative they are if they have a chance to play the role of the generous and understanding neighbor. For instance, you are going to have to remove any trees whose trunks are within twenty feet of the court surface; otherwise, the roots may gradually destroy the court. If the trees are on your neighbors' property, then those neighbors are going to have to be very understanding indeed!

When you are examining the factors affecting the installation of the fence, be forewarned that I will recommend a twelve-foot—not a ten-foot—fence. If zoning or other considerations make the twelve-footer impossible, then a ten-footer will do, but many more balls will go over it. A standard ball will bounce over a ten-foot fence quite often. The twelve-foot fence will stop almost every ball that bounces within the normal course of play.

If there are any aspects of the *where* decision that are still questionable, you may find the answers by going to specific chapters on each aspect of construction.

But by now, I will assume, you have either discovered where you can put the court or you have abandoned the project. For those in the former category, we are ready for the ultimate question: *how?*

The "How To" Principle

"He can do anything with his hands."

"I'm all thumbs."

"He can fix anything."

"I can't even change a light bulb without blowing a fuse."

The twentieth century might well be identified by the proliferation of impersonal mechanical skills required to keep our everyday machinery functioning. Very few households are prepared to deal with the most ordinary mechanical breakdown, even though they depend on numerous machines every day.

In past centuries children began very early to learn the skills that they would need throughout life from their fathers and mothers. Boys learned all the skills of their agricultural life. Girls learned the homemaking skills that kept families fed and clothed. Of course, there were skilled trades, like carpentry and stone-masonry and barrel-making and blacksmithing, but even these were not foreign to farm-raised boys. They had handled stone and wood and learned to keep up fences and mend harness. All these skills were closely associated with their lives.

Today we are surrounded by mechanical contrivances that most people regard as wholly mysterious. Under the automobile hood, behind the enamel façade of the dishwasher, inside the circuit breaker, behind the gleaming eye of the television screen, in every corner of everyday life, there are mechanisms that most people don't dare to investigate.

The fact is, most of the mechanical skills needed to penetrate these mysteries are no more complex than were the ancient mechanical jobs. But there are so many of them, most people simply use the telephone to solve household mechanical break-downs. ("Well, can you come this afternoon? It's leaking all over the kitchen." Pause. "Thursday! We'll all drown by then!")

This book will not tell you how to fix all your mechanical breakdowns. But it may give many of you the courage to deal with some problems you have always regarded with fear. If you read the rest of this chapter trustingly, you may be ready to investigate the cause of and even solve many mechanical problems in your house, in your lawn mower, and even under the hood of your car. At any rate, you *will* have the confidence to build your own tennis court.

Because you may have grown up suffering to some degree from *fear of the machine,* one of my most important aims is to instill *courage*—to make you approach the mechanical unknown with confidence. I was fortunate. In his teens my son James quite fearlessly pulled apart and reassembled automobiles. That im-pressed me. And it made his brothers and me somewhat more daring. Then Don Ackerson gave me the specific tennis-court-building courage—he and the USLTA handbook. And one more factor: Robert M. Pirsig's *Zen and the Art of Motorcycle Maintenance,* which I recommend highly. First, it's a rather extraordinary story of human breakdown and mending. Secondly, in terms of our present preoccupation, it will give you a unique lesson in the pure function of *doing* mechanical things. It quite literally gave me the strength to take apart, clean, and reassemble a carburetor, followed closely by a magneto. From that time on, the world was mine!

Let me explain what I learned from Pirsig. To do anything that involves the use of tools and materials you are not familiar with, you must first understand how the "thing" works. What function does it perform? Why are the various parts needed for it to perform that function? What is the necessary relationship of those parts? In other words, you must understand it as a *whole,* in

The court is in motion in relation to the things around it.

terms of function. Knowing a list of the parts will not tell you that. Knowing that A attaches to B by using C is not enough unless you know *why*.

Pirsig makes it very clear that a numbered list of steps in doing something is in itself inadequate instruction. It is not enough to say, "Do this, then do this, then do this." You must understand that when you put A together with B by using C in a certain position, it will then be useful in a specific function of the whole.

Such understanding takes patience and care, but once achieved, it allows you to approach a job knowing that even if one of the parts is numbered wrong or if a screw is left out or if any number of unexpected situations arise, you will be able to deal with the problems without throwing the whole thing out and starting over.

One job of this book will be to show you how a tennis court "works"—not just to provide step-by-step instruction. I want you to know why you take each step and how all the elements relate.

It may not have occurred to you that a tennis court works, that it is in motion. This will be the first part of the lesson. The court is in motion in relation to the things around it and within it. Water runs under it and across it, and in some cases, through it. Wind blows across it. Sleet, snow, hail, sticks, leaves, feet, and tennis balls all make their assault on the surface. Chemical and physical changes take place around it and within it.

A very substantial form of motion is provided every day throughout the year by changes in humidity and temperature. The earth, rock, gravel, and all the materials of the court expand and contract almost constantly, sometimes several times a day.

Therefore, our objective in building the court will be to provide for the greatest possible stability against this constant motion —to counteract the effects of all these forces, so that the court will retain as far as possible, over a period of many years, those qualities that make it satisfactory for its purpose: tennis. The surface must retain its flatness, as well as uniform density and firmness, so that balls will bounce consistently, and the court must be able to shed water as easily as possible, to make it available for play a maximum number of days and hours during the year.

On to the next question—a much more specific one in terms of tennis.

What Kind of Court?

Assuming you have not been stopped by why, where, or how, we are now ready to ask, "What?" What kind of surface? What kind of material? What kind of court?

Tennis players develop favorites among surfaces, and in recent years the variety of choices has grown almost as fast as the number of players. In considering what court you will build yourself, it would be wise to think not only of your favorite surface but of initial installation difficulty, installation cost, and maintenance time and cost.

There are two broad categories into which all courts may be divided: porous and nonporous.

Porous Courts

The simplest of all courts, of course, is of packed earth, topped perhaps with a layer of clay and/or treated with calcium chloride, so that it will hold moisture better and so be less dusty. Depending on the drainage you provide, it can be quite a satisfactory surface at a minimum cost. Disadvantages are that it dries slowly after rain and requires constant maintenance—that is, treating, rolling, watering.

The porous surface that has, with good reason, gained enormous popularity is crushed crystalline greenstone, with an underlying layer of crushed stone, to permit rapid absorption and drainage of water. Best known among these is Har-Tru.® (See Appendix A.) It is an enormously satisfying surface in several ways: it can be played on shortly after quite heavy rain; it provides a very comfortable surface for the feet and legs; if it is in good condition, it gives a very even, moderately slow bounce; the material moves easily underfoot, permitting you to slide, which reduces the danger of twisting an ankle (but also makes it more difficult to reverse direction quickly); and the ball grips well in the loose material for a spin in any direction (though it skids on a hard, flat shot).

The installation cost of the crushed greenstone surface is moderate, compared to that of the nonporous surfaces, and the skill involved in installation is within the capabilities of the amateur builder, provided care and patience are observed.

Maintenance of the porous surface is an important factor. It must be cared for constantly. You cannot relax the routines of watering, brushing, rolling, and treating. The lines must be taken up each winter and put down in the spring. And in the spring the court must be put in condition before the season can begin. However, if you have the time and willing manpower to take care of the court, the tasks are relatively simple. In areas of the country where there is no frost, the surface can of course be used year round.

Nonporous Courts

In the evolution of the nonporous court, two base materials have been employed generally: cement and asphalt. Cement was used in hot climates because asphalt tended to become soft when the heat was intense. In recent years, however, asphaltic compounds have been improved and are being used successfully in places like Phoenix, Arizona; Southern California; and Florida. And because the asphalt base is highly compatible with newly developed asphaltic-emulsion playing surfaces, it has come into general use for these very popular surfaces. Cement is employed for certain synthetic surfaces utilizing modern plastic technology. These surfaces must be applied by the manufacturer with special equipment and so are not within the scope of this book.

The various materials manufactured for application on top of asphalt fall into two basic categories: cushioned and noncushioned. Within each type are surfaces that vary in price, ease of application, and degree of traction. Some are quite rubbery. Others are soft, while still allowing for a small amount of slide.

Since our objective is to deal with building methods that we can handle ourselves (at least for the most part), I will not suggest materials that require highly specialized equipment or that can only be obtained from and applied by the manufacturer. Among these are, for instance, polyurethane and rubber.

The cost of a nonporous surface utilizing an asphalt base is somewhat higher than for a porous surface. You will need expert help in putting down the asphalt. This is the major difference in the cost and in the difficulty of the job. The maintenance of a nonporous court, however, is far easier. The surface should require virtually no attention for at least five years, except to be kept relatively clean with broom and squeegee when leaves and other materials get on the court. After about five years, depending on the deterioration of the surface and the paint, the court may require a simple resurfacing coat or perhaps only a coat of paint.

The nonporous court can be played on at any time of the year, and if it is flat and the grade is correct, with the help of sun, wind, and/or rolling squeegees, it is ready for play shortly after heavy rain. To help you make a choice among surfaces, there is a comparison of their characteristics in Appendix C.

2.

Time, Muscle, Brain, Money, and Tools

Before you even think of building, you should have a good idea of what you'll need. Apart from the actual materials, you'll have to have certain amounts of time, muscle, brain power, tools, and of course, money. The following pages will help you to plan ahead for all these needs.

Time

Most of the work on your court can be done in short spurts, which means that you don't have to take a month's vacation or quit your job. You can work for a few days and stop, then pick it up again on the next weekend and stop again. And so forth.

Try to plan your time—but don't expect to keep to a strict schedule; you almost certainly won't be able to. Robert Pirsig counsels against the notion that you must finish by any special time. It is more important to work carefully and patiently than to try to meet a deadline. After all, the court will be there for a long time. But once it is finished, you will have a very hard time correcting any errors. (See Appendix E for detailed schedule.)

Phase One

The initial phase is the planning. How long that takes depends on you. It involves such decisions as what kind of court you want, its exact position, how much you should budget for it, and who is going to help you with it.

Phase Two

This is the ground-breaking phase. It involves clearing; removing rocks, trees, and other impediments to the smooth course of your court; and installing whatever drainage facilities you need to keep the court area from holding water. These tasks can be accomplished in all kinds of weather except when the ground is frozen. Damp and cold will not stop you if you can stand them. Therefore, like phase one, this ground-breaking can be scheduled for almost any time of year. I would suggest you do it in the spring or early summer, so that you can follow it closely by phase three.

Phase Three

This phase differs for the porous and the nonporous courts. For the nonporous court it involves laying the rock base. The temperature should be comfortable to work in but it will otherwise have no effect on the work. Moderate amounts of rain will not be harmful. They will simply cost you time because no one wants to work in the rain.

For the porous court this phase is combined with phase four and will include the laying of the stone base and the laying of the crushed greenstone playing surface. Again, moderate temperatures are desirable for working comfort. Moderate rain will cost time but will not injure the materials. However, it would be wise to keep the bags of greenstone from getting wet before spreading them. The material holds moisture well and will be very heavy when wet.

Phase Four (nonporous court only)

This involves laying the asphalt layers. As long as it starts in dry weather, so that you have your first layer down, rain won't hurt you. Once you start, the asphalt should be down in a matter of four or five days—maximum.

Phase Five

Landscaping, seeding, putting up the fence and the net, and for the porous court, putting down lines. For the nonporous court, you can be working while the asphalt is curing. I would advise a minimum of six weeks for the curing and if this carries you into weather below 50 degrees Fahrenheit, you will have to wait for spring before going to phase six. You may, therefore, want to line the court and play winter tennis on the asphalt. The longer curing time will be all to the good.

Phase Six (nonporous court only)

There are two more jobs, and they both require warm, dry weather: spreading the playing surface and applying the tennis-court paint. Fortunately, you can complete both jobs quickly, and it doesn't take long for the surface and paint to dry. You just don't want it to rain before they do.

Muscle, Brain, and Money

Although the schedule presented in Appendix E will help you to plan your time, keep flexible. Remember, you can't build a tennis court alone. You need many helping hands, sympathy, support, and encouragement by those who are near and dear to you. Take careful count of your supporters. Check out your family. You, your family, and friends (especially the tennis players among them) are your primary source of muscle and brain. The more you do without professional help, of course, the more you will save—and the whole purpose of this book is to make it possible for you to have your own tennis court at a price you can afford.

You should employ outside help for short periods of time and only for jobs that require skills and equipment that are beyond your capability. If you follow this rule, you will find that your

Muscle and brain

court may cost 60 to 70 percent less than it would if installed entirely by an outside contractor.

Your greatest saving will come from two areas: the engineering (a job that requires a fairly high degree of brain) and the general labor (jobs that require varying amounts of brain, some of which require a considerable amount of muscle).

Engineering

I probably shouldn't use the word because it may frighten you, unless you happen to be armed with engineering skills or you have someone working with you who is.

It needn't frighten you at all if you will follow the "how to" principle and allow yourself time. Don't let a time schedule rule you. Absorb chapters 3 and 4 before hiring bulldozers or setting your vacation dates at the office.

Since *you* are the contractor on the job—the boss—plan carefully, make simple, neat drawings, as described in the pages to come, and practice with the transit until you find it easy to use.

Above all, don't rush or feel rushed.

General Labor

The man-hours of digging, raking, and hauling will be many. Raking is perhaps the most time- and labor-consuming chore throughout the various stages of construction, and digging is a close second.

Except in a few instances, it is hard to be very specific about the number of workers you will need for each job. For one thing, it will depend on the abilities of your friends and neighbors. Some will be able to do many things well. Others will be useful only for holding the end of a string or raking. The critical jobs will be performed by you and perhaps one or two others who manifest considerable skill and comprehension.

I have no doubt that as you talk about the project in advance, you will attract many volunteers. Once you have them, keep up their enthusiasm by putting them to work when you get them on the job. Have enough tools so that everyone has something to do. If necessary, you can borrow rakes and shovels. Mark them carefully so they can be returned to the right person, and keep the whole job humming.

Finding Professional Help

Draw on the experience of friends or neighbors who have had any sort of work done. If you find a good bulldozer operator—recommended by someone who has used him—he will probably be able to take care of the ditchdigger, bucket-loader, and truck(s). If all else fails, you can try the Yellow Pages.

Discuss the project with any operators you are interested in hiring. Again, don't rush anyone into a decision. You are much more likely to get people interested if you give them time to do the job carefully. Compare prices of at least two operators before deciding what you should pay.

A "good asphalt man" may take you time to find. If you are building a nonporous court, he is a critical element. There are some very skillful contractors who put in driveways and parking lots. But tennis courts require even more painstaking work. Therefore, you must find a man who takes an interest in achieving the degree of perfection you will need. Again, find out his reputation from people who have used him. Describe the project and give him time to decide.

Work Force

THE PROFESSIONALS
   Bulldozer operator
   Ditchdigger operator (if you do not do it by hand)

Bucket-loader operator
Road-scraper operator (if used)
Truckdriver (to deliver stone)
Asphalt-installation crew
Fencing-installation crew (if you do not do it yourself)

The same person may be able to perform more than one of these jobs.

YOU, YOUR FAMILY, AND FRIENDS

(Note: The ratio of brain to muscle is somewhat higher for the jobs at the top of the list and decreases toward the end. Conversely, the need for muscle increases sharply toward the end.

1. Transit operator
2. Someone to draw plans, figure quantities
3. Rod person
4. Someone to mix cement and other materials
5. Carpenter (simple jobs)
6. Painter
7. Digger (pick and shovel)
8. Raker
9. Hauler and lifter
10. Helpers for the jobs listed above

For jobs 7 through 10, you should have three or four helpers, perhaps more, available.

Tools

You will need many tools for a great variety of jobs. Most are fairly simple tools. Many, you can borrow; others, you may have to buy. But remember, the money you spend on them is negligible, considering what you will save on your court. Most of these tools will be familiar objects. Others may be totally alien. Therefore, I will discuss the use of the less common ones as though you knew nothing about them.

Like the list of workers, the list below begins with those tools that involve the highest ratio of brain to muscle and ends with those that require the greatest amount of muscle. But please bear in mind that there is some skill involved in the use of any tool. Parenthetical numbers following certain entries indicate the quantity needed. You will find many of the tools illustrated in Figure 1.

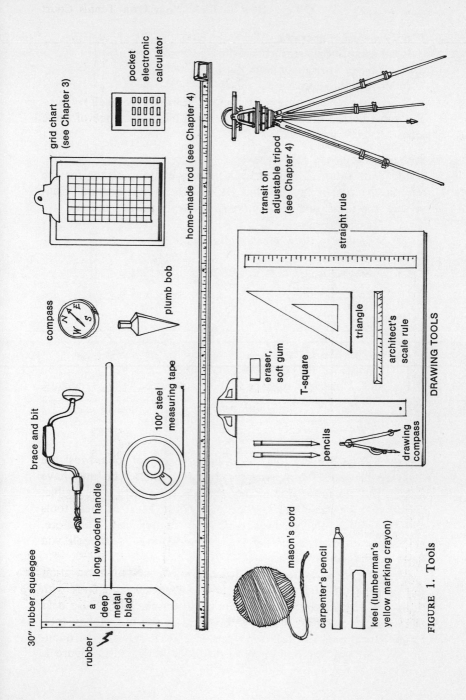

FIGURE 1. Tools

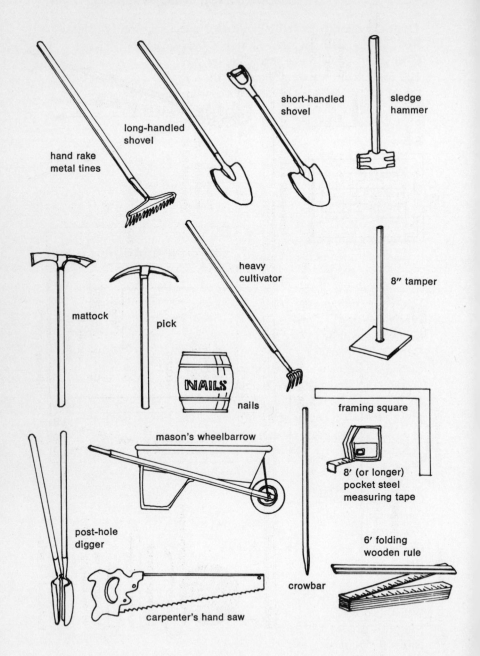

hand rake
metal tines

long-handled
shovel

short-handled
shovel

sledge
hammer

mattock

pick

heavy
cultivator

8″ tamper

nails

mason's wheelbarrow

framing square

8′ (or longer)
pocket steel
measuring tape

post-hole
digger

6′ folding
wooden rule

crowbar

carpenter's hand saw

Transit, engineering or builder's (for specifics, see Chapter 3)
Rod, home-made, in feet and inches (see Chapter 3)
Grid chart, home-made (see Chapter 3)
100-foot steel measuring tapes (2)
8-foot (or longer) pocket steel measuring tapes (6)
6-foot folding wooden rule
Pocket electronic calculator
Drawing tools
  Drawing board
  T-square
  Triangle
  Pencils
  Erasers, good grade
  Drawing compass
  12-inch ruler or
    straightedge
  Scale rule
Compass (unless your transit has one)
Plumb bob
Chalked snapline
Carpenter's pencil
Keel (lumberman's yellow marking crayon)
Wooden stakes, 1 x 2-inch pine (44)
Ball of good, heavy cotton cord
Power tools (you can use hand tools, but power tools make it
  easier if you have them available):
  Skilsaw
  Jig saw
  Drill
Carpenter's hammer
Carpenter's hand saw
Framing square
Carpenter's level
Brace and bit
Tin snips
2-inch paintbrushes (2)
Whisk broom
Big push broom
Nails, tacks, screws (various sizes)
30-inch rubber squeegees, long-handled, with deep blades (2)

Mason's wheelbarrows (2 or 3)
Mason's trowels (2 or 3)
Hoes (2)
Small sledge hammer
Large sledge hammer
8-inch tamper
Post-hole digger (2 or 3 if you are doing your own fence)
Pick (or 2)
Mattock (or 2)
Crowbar
Long-handled shovels (2 or 3)
Short-handled shovels (2)
Spade
Metal hand rakes (3 or 4)
Heavy cultivators (2)
13-foot scaffolding boards (4)

Cost Estimate Outline

It would be folly to try to tell you how much it will cost you to build a court. It could only be done by knowing when and where you are going to build, what special problems you face because of the site, and what local costs will be for materials, services, and professional labor. A hundred miles or a hundred days could change the figures substantially.

The major cost factors, which can be estimated by getting prices from local contractors and suppliers, are as follows:

PHASES ONE AND TWO
Bulldozer and other heavy equipment, by the hour or day
Transit rental, by the month
Any tools you must purchase

PHASES THREE AND FOUR (porous)
Sprinkler-system materials
Plumbing contractor (if needed)
Brick, cement, sand, lumber (curb and screed strips)
Motor roller, by the hour or day
Crushed rock and screenings for base, by the ton
40 tons of fast-dry material

PHASE THREE (nonporous)
Rock base, by the ton
Bulldozer or road-scraper for leveling, by the hour
Motor roller, by the hour or day

PHASE FOUR (nonporous)
Asphalt contract
Lumber for net-post plugs

PHASE FIVE
Net posts, cement, sand
Fencing materials (if you do it yourself)
Fencing contractor (if needed)
Landscaping
 Bulldozer, trucks (if needed)
 Grass seed, fertilizer
Court line paint

PHASE SIX (nonporous)
Playing-surface material and color coat
Patching material
Squeegees

Itemized Estimate

In Appendix B I have itemized the cost of my own court and provided space for you to fill in your estimated figures—which will, in most cases, be a good deal higher because prices have risen considerably since we built. But my figures will at least give you some idea of the relative costs involved.

I have also included figures for a porous court, although I have not built one; I know others who have, and I was able to get comparative costs. As you will see, porous courts can be done less expensively. The cost of fencing varies a great deal, depending on the type you choose. Other costs will be much the same, no matter what kind of court you build. You should not skimp on the rock base or the drainage. Lower prices are a justifiable goal—but lower standards in the specifications will bring you grief within a few years.

3.

Engineering

We are ready to decide exactly where the court will lie, how it will face the sun, what its dimensions will be, and how much grade it will have. These decisions will guide everyone in helping you build the court, and they will determine to a great extent its durability and the enjoyment it will give all who play on it.

Our first job will be to create a detailed layout for the court. Then we will create a tool that we will have with us through the entire job. I have named it the grid chart. The following list should give you an idea of what you'll need for the engineering.

Tools

Drawing tools
    Drawing board
    T-square
    Triangle
    Scale rule
    Drawing compass
    Pencils
    Erasers, good grade
100-foot steel measuring tapes (2)

Compass (unless transit has one)
Wooden stakes, 1 by 2 by 12 inches (44)
Small nails
Hammer, carpenter's
Ball of good heavy, cotton cord
Grid chart (described on pages 39–40)

Work Force

You
2 helpers (from time to time)

Time

2 days minimum (be flexible)

The Layout

There are three determinations to make in the layout of the court: the placement of the court in relation to the north-south axis, the area that it will occupy, and its grade, or slant.

North-South Orientation

Most experts have come to agree that the most satisfactory orientation for a court is on the north-south axis. This is true over virtually the whole of the United States.

The seasons are caused by the inclination of the earth's axis in relation to its orbit around the sun. The inclination, or tilt, is 23.5 degrees from the vertical. This means that in the northern hemisphere, there is a 47 degree difference in the height of the sun above the horizon at noon from June 21 to December 21 (see Figure 2). In summer the sun is relatively high in the sky during the middle of the day. If your court runs directly north and south, then at midday the player on the north end of the court will be looking *under* the sun—not *into* it—at most of the balls he receives. Early and late in the day, when the sun is low, it will be far to the side of the player and out of his or her vision for the majority of shots.

However, in winter, particularly in the more northerly parts of the United States, the sun never gets very high above the horizon. This means that at noon the sun is directly in your line of vision for

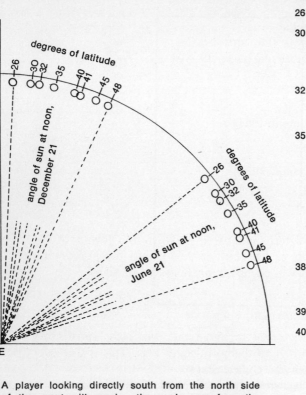

A player looking directly south from the north side of the court will receive the sun's rays from the angle indicated by the degree of latitude for the location of the court. Point E is the player's eye. You can see how difficult it is to escape the sun in Seattle at midday on June 21.

FIGURE 2. Highest and lowest angles of the sun in a range of cities

Degrees of Latitude	City
26	Miami, Fla.
30	Houston, Tex. Jacksonville, Fla. New Orleans, La. St. Augustine, Fla.
32	Dallas, Tex. Hilton Head, S.C. Savannah, Ga.
35	Albuquerque, N.Mex. Amarillo, Tex. Atlanta, Ga. Charlotte, N.C. Chattanooga, Tenn. Little Rock, Ark. Los Angeles, Calif. Memphis, Tenn. Oklahoma City, Okla. Phoenix, Ariz.
38	Richmond, Va. San Francisco, Calif. St. Louis, Mo.
39	Washington, D.C.
40	Columbus, Ohio Denver, Colo. Indianapolis, Ind. Kansas City, Mo. Philadelphia, Penn. Pittsburgh, Penn. Reno, Nev.
41	Chicago, Ill. Des Moines, Iowa New York, N.Y. Omaha, Neb. Salt Lake City, Utah
42	Boston, Mass. Cleveland, Ohio Toledo, Ohio
45	Bangor, Maine Montreal, Can. Minneapolis, Minn. Pierre, S.D. Portland, Ore.
48	Seattle, Wash.

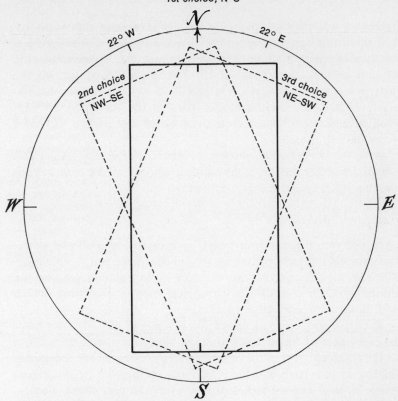

FIGURE 3. The second choice, 22 degrees northwest to southeast, is a good first choice in southern latitudes.

many of the high shots in the north court. There are times in winter tennis when you feel there is no way to escape the sun when you serve. This is particularly true in the midafternoon and late afternoon for a right-handed player in the north court.

In the southerly latitudes, the sun is considerably higher throughout the year. The USTA manual, among others, suggests that you turn the court as much as 22 degrees off the north-south axis, toward the northwest-southeast axis, if your court is south of the forty-second parallel (see Figure 3). This is not wise, in my opinion. The whole theory depends on the assumption that you are more likely to play tennis during the latter part of the day than during the early hours. However, if you are left-handed and you like to play at eight A.M., turning the court 22 degrees to the southeast will be very annoying on the serve and the overhead.

I think this can be a practical solution farther south—perhaps south of the thirty-sixth or thirty-seventh parallel. There you would be able to make better use of the late afternoon by turning the players away from the late, low sun. And because the sun is relatively higher through the earlier part of the day, you are still looking under it for most shots even at ten A.M., when the court faces the sun directly.

Still, for general play during all hours of the day, America's players, whether left- or right-handed, will not make a mistake if they put their courts on the north-south axis.

Compass Correction

In order to lay out your court by compass, you should determine the compass correction for true north where you are building. A phone call to your county engineer's office should get you the information. Or consult a topographical map of your area, which will indicate the correction needed.

In either case, compass correction is made in the following way: In every area of the country, there is what is called a declination of the compass. This is the number of degrees by which a compass reading in your area will be at variance, or *decline* from the true north. If, as is true in much of the northeastern part of the country, the declination is a number of degrees west, that means your

FIGURE 4. When the compass declination is 12 degrees west, this means that magnetic north is 12 degrees west of true north. For true north, read 12 degrees east of magnetic north.

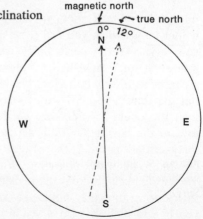

compass is pointing to the west of true north. So you must correct your reading by that number of degrees in an easterly direction. For example, suppose your county engineer says, "In your location, the declination of the compass is 12 degrees west" (see Figure 4). Then you will find true north by reading the number of degrees of declination (12) in the opposite direction (east) of your actual compass reading, thus compensating for the "error."

If your information is that the declination of the compass is zero, then of course, magnetic north and true north are the same in your location and no correction needs to be made. The line of zero declination runs down through Lake Michigan, Michigan, Indiana, Kentucky, western North Carolina, South Carolina, and into the Caribbean Sea.

The farther west you go of that zero declination line, the greater the degree of declination east. Conversely, the farther east you are of that line, the greater the degree of declination west (see declination map, Figure 5).

An 11- or 12-degree error between magnetic and true north could make a considerable difference in the positioning of your court. If you are one of those people who can pick out the North

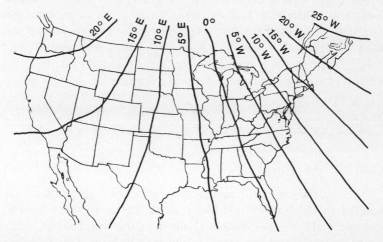

FIGURE 5. Compass declinations. *U.S. Department of Commerce, Environmental Sciences Services Administration, Coast and Geodetic Survey*

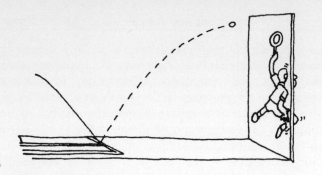

There *are* top-spin lobs that require even greater depth—but we must compromise somewhere . . .

Star (Polaris) at the end of the handle of the Little Dipper (Ursa Minor), you can make a sighting at night and put some stakes in the ground to indicate true north. This will be accurate enough.

If you are still in doubt about what direction to choose, I suggest you take some time on a sunny day to experiment. Lay out a tape or string for a baseline at right angles to the north-south axis and stand on the baseline facing south. Try tossing a ball up for a serve; then toss one up for an overhead stroke and make a note in each case of how the sun may affect play using the north-south axis. Then turn your portable baseline 22 degrees or less toward the southeast. Go through the same ball-toss exercises and make more notes. Repeat this procedure every two hours.

You may have to compromise the ideal direction for the court because of zoning regulations, property lines, or unalterable physical factors. I urge you to do everything you can to resist turning the court very far from the north-south axis. But I guess we will all admit that *any* direction is better than no court at all.

Area of the Court

The area the court will occupy may affect your decision on the direction in which you would like it to lie. Let us consider the area now and make a final decision about both the direction and area.

The dimensions of the court should be 120 by 60 feet (see Figure 6). This is 7,200 square feet, or just under ⅙ acre. Anything larger is an unnecessary luxury; anything smaller should be con-

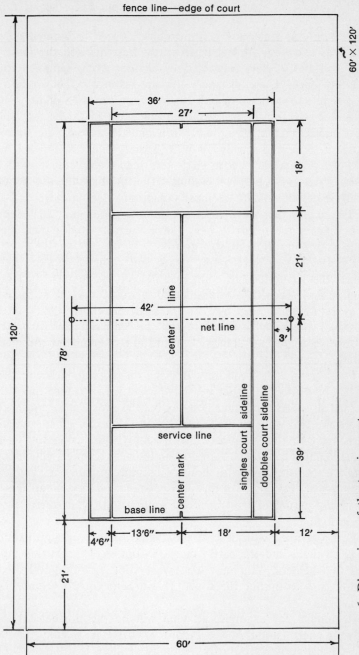

FIGURE 6. Dimensions of the tennis court

sidered only as a necessary compromise. These recommended dimensions allow for 21 feet between the baseline and the fence at each end and 12 feet between the sidelines of the doubles court and the fence. These distances are not arbitrary. They relate to the height and distance of ball bounce from the area of play—the 78 foot by 36 foot area in which a ball must hit to be "in," plus the distance that a player must run outside the playing lines in order to retrieve a legally hit ball. Twenty-one feet at each end of the court and 12 feet at each side seems ample in almost all cases. There *are* top-spin lobs that hit on the baseline and require even greater depth but we must compromise somewhere and the USTA advises that the 21-foot margin is a good point at which to stop. Experience seems to have borne out this advice over many years and many thousands of courts.

For those who have ample space and want to indulge themselves, the championship court is 130 feet by 66 feet. Just bear in mind that you will be adding 1,380 square feet worth of material to everything you must buy for the standard court. That's an increase of almost 20 percent. If you are building your own court to save thousands of dollars, I would not recommend the championship court.

I will assume that you have decided on the standard court size of 120 by 60 feet and that you have room for it to face in a satisfactory direction. You must now lay out the prospective court area. There are two ways to make this layout. You can do it with tape measures and thus eliminate the need to begin using the transit immediately. Or you can turn now to the next chapter, which deals with the transit, and learn how to use the instrument. The tape measures are adequate for this part of the job; and you can shorten the rental period of the transit by waiting until you start clearing the ground.

Equip yourself with at least six stakes, a heavy enough hammer to drive them into the earth, two 100-foot steel measuring tapes, and two helpers. You may also want your ball of good, heavy cotton cord to outline the court. It will help you to visualize the area.

Beginning, for example, at what will be the northeast corner of your court (point A; see Figure 7), drive in a stake. (I have chosen this corner arbitrarily. Actually, if there is a barrier which

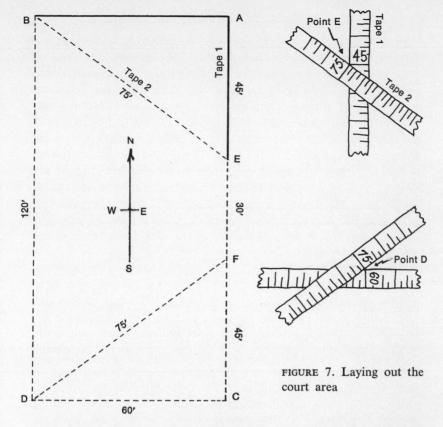

FIGURE 7. Laying out the court area

must be avoided, you might start with the corner stake nearest to it.) Holding your compass directly over the stake, make your compass correction and direct a helper to put in another stake (point B) sixty feet to the west of point A.

With the line A–B you have tentatively established one end of the court. Now measure 120 feet from point A at right angles to line A–B. If you want to be sure you are at right angles, follow this simple geometric principle:

Have one of your helpers hold a tape measure at point A (tape 1); the other should hold a tape at point B (tape 2). Bring the tapes together at the spot where tape 1 measures 45 feet and tape 2 measures 75 feet. At the point where they cross, drive in a stake (point E). The line established by A–E will be at right angles to line A–B. Having established the line A–E, use your tapes and stakes and helpers to extend the line to points F and C. With the

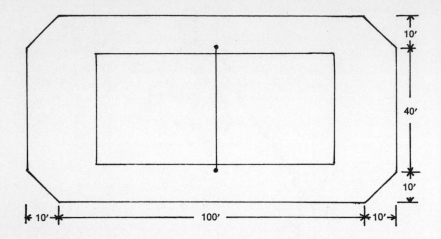

FIGURE 8. Angling corners

tapes held at F and C, you can then find point D, where the tapes
cross. Measure 60 feet with the C–D tape and cross this with the
F–D tape at the 75-foot measurement. (Figure 7 will guide you.)

If you have to shift the position of the court because of an immovable obstacle, you have several choices: shift the court position
away from the obstacle but keep the same north-south direction,
turn the court in a new direction to avoid the obstacle, or reduce
the size of the court. Of these three, the first is the most desirable
and the third is by far the least desirable. If the obstacle intrudes
only slightly in the corner of the court, you could angle your fence
corners as I show in Figure 8. This may eliminate the problem of
the obstacle or at least, make it necessary to move the court only
slightly. The cut-off corner design has been used by many people
quite satisfactorily. It has virtually no effect on play because the
court area that it eliminates is almost never used. This fourth alternative is unquestionably preferable to reducing the overall length
and/or width of the court.

At this point you are ready to make a final decision about the
actual area the court will occupy and its north-south orientation.
I would suggest that you recheck your corner stakes, driving nails
in the tops of the stakes to mark the measurement exactly. And
again, it might be wise to outline the court with white cotton cord,
so that it will be easy to visualize the area.

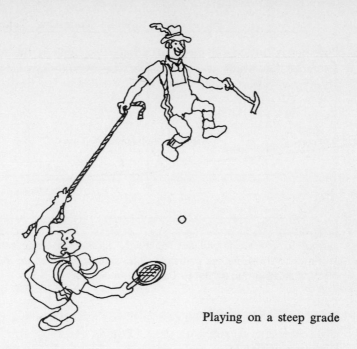

Playing on a steep grade

The Grade

With area and the position of the court established, the final layout consideration is the grade of the court.

The porous court should have a very slight grade to prevent the material from washing. All water should drain *through* the court except in very heavy rain. On the other hand, the nonporous court needs enough of a grade so that all the water will run off but not so much as to affect play.

The recommended grade for porous courts is 1 inch in 20 to 24 feet—in other words, a total grade of 2½ to 3 inches from one side of the 60-foot court to the other. For nonporous courts the recommended grade is 1 inch in every 10 feet or 6 inches from one side of the court to the other. This grade provides for drainage without being so steep that it affects the play. A steeper grade might make you feel as if you were playing on the side of a hill; a slighter one would be less successful in emptying the court of water after a rain. One inch in 10 feet is equal to ¼ inch in every 30 inches. If you have a depression in the court that is 30 inches wide and ¹⁄₁₆ inch deep (see Figure 9), virtually all the water will flow out of it and off the court. Since $\frac{1}{16}$ inch is the allowable tolerance for which we will strive, you should have few if any "birdbaths" after a rain.

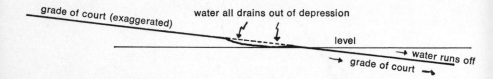

FIGURE 9. The grade and the "birdbath" have been exaggerated about 16 times to illustrate the principle. The actual grade of the nonporous court, 1:120, is too slight to be illustrated here.

Direction of Grade

The grade for both porous and nonporous courts should run from side to side. Any other grading will adversely affect the play.

I have played on one court which was graded downward from the net toward each end. It was the correct grade of 1 inch in ten feet. But it meant that the center of the court was 6 inches higher than each base line. Everyone was hitting uphill. Another grading I have seen was from end to end, for a total difference of almost a foot. One player was always hitting uphill and the other downhill.

Hitting uphill from both ends

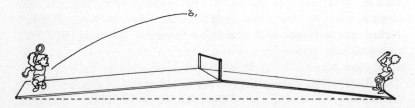

A court graded from one end to the other makes you feel slightly dwarfed. The proper grade from side to side is imperceptible.

The Grid Chart

There is a simple tool you must create to use in conjunction with the transit throughout the construction of the court. The grid chart is nothing more than a plan of the court on which you will record the measurements you obtain with the transit. Here's how to make your grid chart:

Make a plan of the court with your scale rule, using ⅛ inch to 1 foot. (I suggest this scale because it produces a chart of about 17 x 9 inches, which is easy to carry around but big enough for detailed notations.) Mount the grid chart on a large clipboard or piece of plywood—*and have it with you on the job at all times.* Be sure to use a good grade of drawing paper, so that you can erase pencil notations over and over again. In ink, draw the court outline (15 inches by 7½ inches for 120 feet by 60 feet) and then draw a 1¼-inch grid within the court to indicate the 10-foot squares (see Figure 10). This will give you twelve squares for the length of the court and six squares for the width. You will then make notations at each appropriate grid point (where the lines cross), which will correspond to the measurements you make on the court site using the transit and the stakes you will install all around the court (see Figure 12).

FIGURE 10. The grid chart

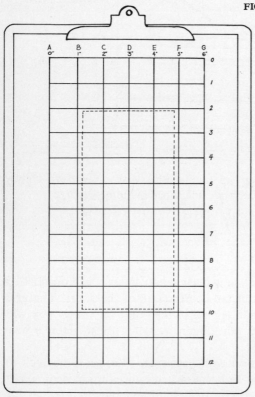

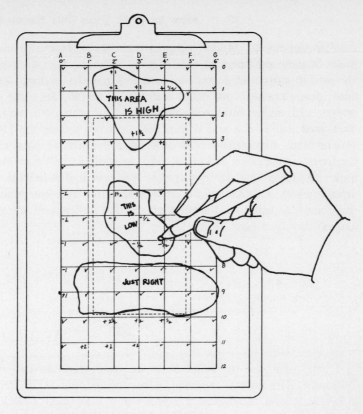

FIGURE 11. Marking low and high points

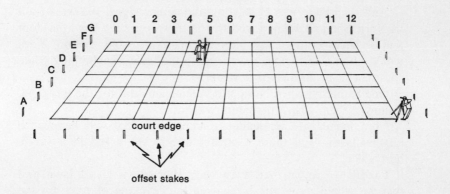

FIGURE 12. Offset stakes around the court

Whoever assists you when you are checking levels of the court must become practiced in sighting the stakes, lengthwise up and down the court and across the court. To make sighting quicker and more accurate, put large numbers or letters on each stake so you can easily direct your assistant to the grid point you want measured.

The method of measuring is covered in the next chapter. For an example of what this looks like on paper when you have marked low and high points, see Figure 11. You will find it helpful to set up some sort of high stand or table beside your transit to hold your grid chart, a pencil, and a good eraser that will not rough up the paper.

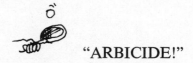

"ARBICIDE!"

I had some bad moments once we were ready to call in the bulldozer. The grass was growing beautifully, the apple tree was flourishing, and there was a silver birch that good friends had given us for our twenty-fifth—silver—wedding anniversary.

All that was inside the lines we had drawn for the court area . . .

And then there was Nora, our middle son's girl. We were fond of Nora. She and Jamie loved to run down over the lawn barefoot and lie back on the grassy slope at midday to soak up sun. Nora would often do her yoga exercises on the lawn—sunbathing while she went from posture to posture.

One Saturday, when Nora and Jamie came out for the weekend, I showed them where the court was to be.

Nora looked at me, seeing a monster. "What will happen to all that lawn—and those beautiful trees?" she asked in a small, hurt voice.

I tried to explain that there was, after all, a lot of lawn and that we would move the birch tree to the circle of trees by the pond and that the apple tree was old. "Apple trees don't live very long," I said, hoping to soften the blow. This was not helpful. After all, the apple tree was *alive,* and I was killing it.

Jamie was silent. He sympathized with Nora's feelings. But he also understood something of what was driving me.

Nora didn't come out to the country while we were building the court, and I did have some twinges of conscience. The look I'd seen in her eyes made me remember how often I had railed against Detroit and Washington for conspiring to cover the world with highways. And here I was, paving over 7,200 square feet of living, breathing earth.

And then I heard the sound of tennis balls bouncing, and I quickly regained my sense of balance. I gassed up the chain saw without a twinge.

4.

The Transit

The most important characteristics of a tennis court are that it be flat and that the flat plane be tipped just enough to drain efficiently. The one instrument which will help you achieve those qualities with great accuracy is the engineering transit.

In one of my early telephone conversations with Don Ackerson, he said, quite as a matter of course, that I would need a transit for the job. In the euphoria I was experiencing at the prospect of having a court, I accepted the fact without really understanding the full significance of his advice. As I progressed further in my plans and talked again to Don, I realized that *someone* would have to be present at all times during the building of the court to operate a transit—and that someone was going to have to be *me*. At every stage of construction the transit is needed to keep a check on the flatness and on the grade—and if your reason for building the court yourself is to save money, you can't afford to have an engineer working for you full time.

I rented a transit by the month, bought a textbook, did some practicing, and found it relatively simple to perform the few transit functions needed for the job.

The purpose of this chapter is once again to save you the trial and error and the searching that I faced. When you've finished this chapter, you won't be able to survey roads and properties and hire yourself out to engineering firms. But fortunately, you don't have to learn *that* much about the transit. I'm just going to teach you what you have to know to build your court because, frankly, that's about all *I* know.

The transit is an ancient and beautiful instrument. Essentially, it's a telescope with cross hairs in the lens and adjustments that make it possible to make the telescope absolutely level. In addition, the instrument has very precise scales so that you can measure angles with great accuracy. And those are the two functions you will use in building the court. You will be able to determine nearly perfect levels and right angles.

Now that you have chosen the area and orientation of the court, the transit can be put to use in checking the relative levels of the ground in and around the court area. You will then have some idea of how much earth will have to be moved in order to achieve the flat, slightly inclined plane of the subbase for the court.

Acquiring a Transit

Ask your friends and neighbors if they can recommend a surveyor they have used and liked. Or perhaps you know of one. Ask him whether he has a transit that he could rent you. If not, ask him if he knows of a good rental place. If that fails, look in the Yellow Pages under "Surveying Instruments." That's where I got my transit. Rent yours by the month.

You may have, among your relatives or friends, a young engineering student who would love to practice by operating the transit for you. The only problem is that he will have to be available at all times when you are working on the court.

The Tripod

A folding wooden tripod is used to support the transit (see Figure 13). If you are given a choice, I suggest the kind with adjustable legs, so that you can use it with ease, no matter what your height. The adjustable tripod is also somewhat easier to set up on irregular or hilly ground.

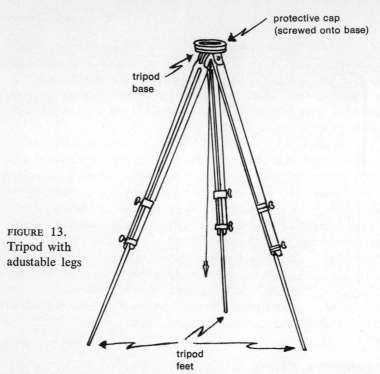

protective cap
(screwed onto base)

tripod
base

FIGURE 13.
Tripod with
adustable legs

tripod
feet

Setting Up the Tripod

Extend the tripod legs and tighten the adjustment screws. Then, moving the legs inward or outward from the center axis (dotted line, Figure 13), make the base as level as possible. If you are unsure about this procedure the first time, you can lay a carpenter's level across the top of the tripod to check. But remember, the tripod doesn't have to be exactly level. The leveling screws on the transit itself will take care of considerable error. The tripod just has to be level enough so that the leveling screws can finish the job. After you've been through the procedure once or twice, you will find it easy.

Be sure all your leg-adjustment screws are tight and that the tripod feet are all pushed *firmly into the ground*. Unscrew the protective cap from the tripod if it has one.

Mounting the Transit on the Tripod

Whether rented or borrowed, the transit will probably come to you in a wooden box. It will be standing upright, screwed onto

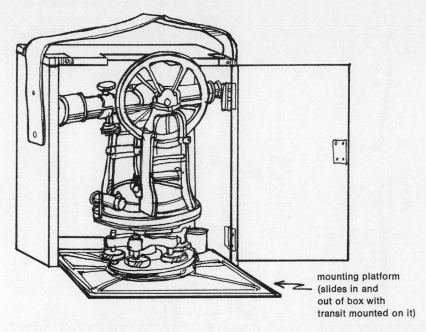

mounting platform
(slides in and
out of box with
transit mounted on it)

FIGURE 14. The transit in its box

a holding plate similar to the one on the tripod (see Figure 14).
Before sliding the transit out of the box, you should loosen or free
the telescope, so that if it bumps anything, it will move freely.
If held rigid, it is in more danger of being damaged. To free the
transit, loosen the telescope clamp screw and the lower clamp
screw, indicated in Figure 15. Now grasp the standards (S) and
slide the transit, attached to its platform, out of the box. You
can now unscrew the transit from the platform, using one hand
to turn the bottom of the transit counterclockwise and the other
hand to support the transit by grasping one of the standards. Now
carry the transit to the tripod and carefully seat it on the threads.
Let the small brass chain drop down through the hole in the
tripod base. Continuing to hold the transit with one hand, carefully thread it onto the tripod base with the other hand. Take
your time and be sure it is threaded smoothly. If it is cross-
threaded, do not force it! Gently back up, going back and forth
with the threads until the two parts thread smoothly. Tighten
gently.

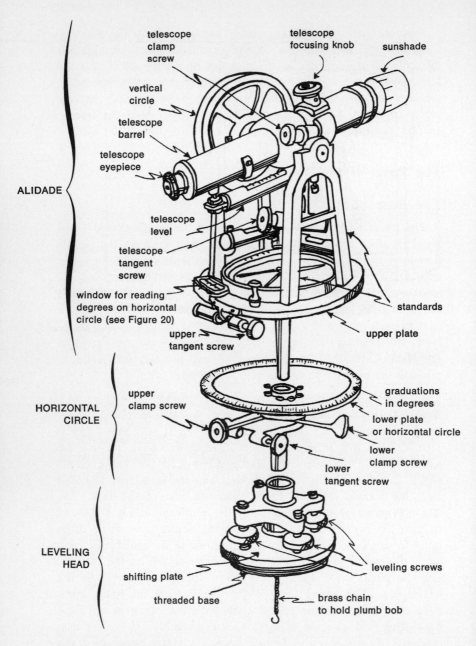

FIGURE 15. The transit

Now that you have the instrument set up, remove the lens cap from the telescope and put on the sunshade. Look through the telescope. Is it necessary to stoop or get up on tiptoe? If it is too high, you may lower it by the leg adjustments or by spreading the legs somewhat. If it is too low, raise it by bringing the legs closer together. While doing this, have a helper hold the transit, so that you won't accidentally tip it over.

The Parts of the Transit

The Base of the Transit

The lower portion of the transit, called the leveling head (Figure 15), does two jobs for us: it levels the transit by the use of four large, brass leveling screws, and it positions the transit exactly over a point on the ground below. When the leveling screws are loosened, the whole upper part of the transit may be slid around on the shifting plate. Try it. Grasp two leveling screws that are next to each other and loosen them both just enough to free them. Now, still holding them, try sliding the transit about on the shifting plate. Carefully please. (Later we will use this procedure to position the plumb bob over a tack in a stake.)

The Middle of the Transit

This area is called the horizontal circle. With the lower clamp screw loosened, the circle is free of the leveling head and can be turned easily.

The Top of the Transit

The top has an impressive name: the alidade. It holds the telescope, the compass, and two levels. With the upper clamp screw loosened, the alidade can turn free of the horizontal circle. Figure 15 shows how the three parts would look if separated.

Leveling

The transit is useless unless it is level at all times. Everything the instrument does is based on the use of gravity to achieve a nearly perfect level. Each time we make a new measurement or move the transit to a new position, we have a constant to make our measurements relate to one another—the direction of gravity.

Leveling the Transit

I am assuming that you loosened the lower clamp screw (see Figure 15) when you removed the transit from its box. If not, loosen it now and also loosen the upper clamp screw. They need only be loose enough so that the circle and the alidade can be turned independently of each other and of the leveling head.

Stand facing the transit at a point where it is easiest for you to grasp two *opposite* leveling screws with the thumb and forefinger of each hand (see Figure 16). Loosen one screw slightly, just enough to make it turn easily. (They all loosen and tighten in the same direction—that is, loosen counterclockwise, tighten clockwise.) Rotate the alidade to bring one of the leveling bubbles around to face you. Now you will be able to observe how far off level the bubble is. Grasp the two leveling screws again and turn them in *opposite* directions, tightening one and loosening

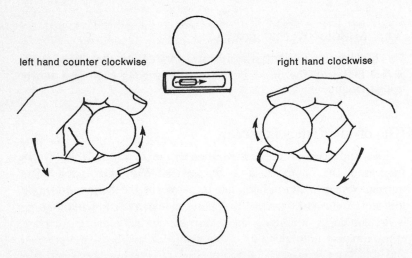

left hand counter clockwise   right hand clockwise

FIGURE 16. Moving the bubble to the right with the leveling screws

the other, to center the bubble. If you want the bubble to move to your right, then you should tighten with your right hand and loosen with your left. If you want the bubble to go to the left, then you should do just the opposite. Be patient. Practice the maneuver slowly. You will probably move the bubble too far and have to reverse the process several times before you have the bubble centered. When it's level, then gently tighten *both* knobs so they are just *snug*—not too tight. As you tighten, you will have to watch the bubble carefully and keep it centered.

Next, move around to face the other two leveling screws on the side where you also face the other bubble level. Repeat the whole procedure.

Now go back to the first bubble. You will probably find that it has been thrown off by leveling the second one. You will have to go back and forth between the two bubbles, leveling each time, until you have achieved a level in both at once. The first time you do it, it may take quite a while, but it will get easier and easier for you each time you set up the transit.

Recheck the Level

The transit will go out of level while you are working with it. This is a normal problem, since the ground will give a little more under one leg than another and the sun's heat will expand the metal of the transit on one side and throw it off level. So you must recheck your level periodically as you use the instrument. It is a good practice to recheck every time you come back to the transit from some other task.

Use of the Tangent Screws

You will notice that with each of the three clamp screws (see Figures 15 and 19) there is an associated tangent screw. The tangent screws make it possible to make very exact settings of the motions of the transit. To make an exact setting, the setting is first made by loosening the clamp screw and moving the parts approximately into position. The clamp screw is then tightened and exact positioning is accomplished by turning the associated tangent screw.

As each function of the transit is described, the use of the clamp screws and tangent screws involved will be described. The lower tangent screw will be used to make exact horizontal positioning of the alidade possible. In effect, this is used when looking through the telescope and exactly positioning the telescope horizontally.

The upper tangent screw is used to position the alidade in relation to the horizontal circle. The position is read on the horizontal scale.

The telescope tangent screw is used to make exact vertical settings of the telescope. These are made either by the vertical scale, the telescope level, or by visual sighting through the telescope, depending on what you are doing.

Just remember, to make an exact setting, the clamp screw must be tightened before the associated tangent screw is operative.

The Telescope

Before leveling the telescope with the telescope tangent screw, it should be focused by the person who will be using it.

Loosen the telescope clamp screw (see Figure 19) and point the telescope toward open sky. Grasp the telescope eyepiece between thumb and forefinger and revolve it while looking through the eyepiece. The object is to bring the cross hairs (see Figure 17A) into sharp focus. If the telescope is equipped with stadia hairs (see Figure 17B), turn the eyepiece back and forth until you see only the cross hairs. For our purposes, the stadia hairs are unnecessary and will only be confusing. Bear in mind, different operators of the transit with different vision may have to refocus on the cross hairs to suit their eyesight.

Leveling the Telescope

This is a simple operation but even more delicate than leveling the lower part of the transit. It is no more important, of course, because if the transit as a whole is not level, leveling the telescope is a waste of time. Therefore, always check the level of the transit before leveling the telescope.

For guidance in this operation, look at Figure 19. Loosen the telescope clamp screw and watching the vertical scale, push the

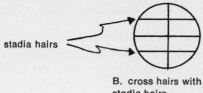 

stadia hairs

B. cross hairs with
stadia hairs

A. simple cross hairs

FIGURE 17. Looking through the eyepiece

telescope barrel up or down to bring the V mark on the scale to the zero mark. The telescope will now be approximately level. Tighten the telescope clamp screw and turn the telescope tangent screw to center the bubble in the telescope level.

As with the transit leveling, recheck the telescope level periodically during use.

Horizontal Settings

Next, we will set the alidade in relation to the horizontal circle. To make this setting we will use the horizontal scale (see Figure 18). If your transit has two horizontal scales, you may use either one or the other for our purposes. I will simply refer to "the horizontal scale."

With the upper and lower clamp screws loosened, look at the horizontal scale and bring the V into alignment with the zero as nearly as you can by quick adjustment. Then tighten the upper clamp screw and using a magnifying glass, turn the upper tangent screw until the V and the zero are in exact alignment.

What you may notice (see Figure 19) is that the lines to either side of the zero do not line up with those on the outer graduated scale. This is the reason: the inner circle is called a vernier scale and its purpose is to make it possible to make settings or take readings which are smaller than the smallest divisions on the outer scale. We will not need to use this capability. We are only concerned with making simple settings. Therefore, you will always line up the zero point with the desired graduation on the outer scale.

Compass Settings

With the lower clamp screw still loosened, and the upper clamp screw tightened, we will now set the telescope on the north-south

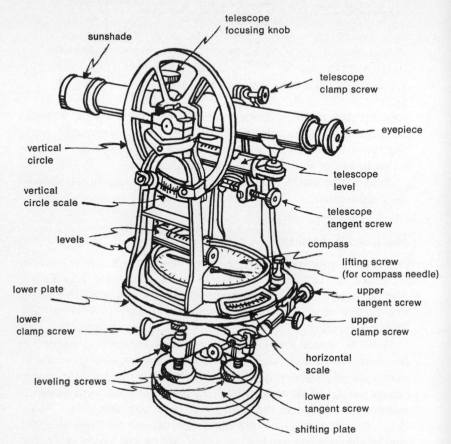

FIGURE 18. The transit from left side showing vertical circle scale

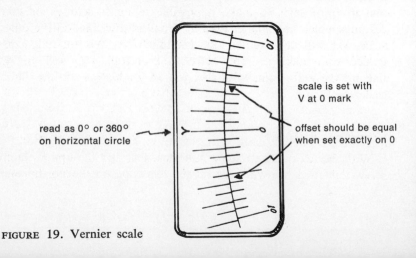

FIGURE 19. Vernier scale

axis by means of the compass, making correction for true north.

To free the compass needle so it can float and settle toward north, loosen the compass needle lifting screw (see Figure 18). When loosened, it allows a small arm to drop away from the needle, thus freeing the needle. Experiment with this by tightening and loosening and watching the interaction of the little arm and the needle.

With the compass needle free, let it settle completely toward magnetic north. If you are uncertain about north and south, you will notice that a small counterweight of wire is wound around the south end of the compass needle.

Turn the horizontal circle so that the compass scale is aimed at true north. (To do this, make the compass correction described on pages 30–33.) Now tighten the lower clamp screw, locking the transit on the north-south axis.

Using the Transit for Layout

Even though you have already learned how to lay out the court and stake the corners by the use of two tape measures (pages 32–36), I would suggest you practice "shooting the stakes" with the transit (you'll learn how later in this chapter). If the transit is set up and used carefully, it will be more precise over irregular ground than the tape method alone; the instrument has the advantage of being unaffected by the contours of the ground, since it makes sightings through the air. Therefore, if the area of the court slopes steeply or is very irregular, it would be wise to recheck your layout with the transit. If the area of the court is relatively flat and smooth to begin with, the tape-measure system is accurate enough.

In the previous chapter you drove corner stakes in laying out the court area. In addition to these we will now drive two offset stakes off each corner (see Figure 20). The purpose of the offset stakes is to delineate the boundaries of the court without interfering with work being done in the actual court area. When the bulldozer comes in to move rocks, trees, and earth, the corner stakes will have to be removed and the offset stakes will be used to guide the work. The distance separating the offset stake from its corner stake can vary depending on the need. If you have to move a great deal of earth, you may need to place the offset stakes more than fifteen feet from each corner. Once you have practiced the use of the transit, you will find it easy to shoot new stake positions when needed.

Setting Up Transit Over a Point

You can begin with any corner stake that is convenient. In Figure 20, I begin with point A. If you have not placed a small tack or finishing nail in corner stake A, do so now. You will make

FIGURE 20. Placing offset and corner stakes, using transit

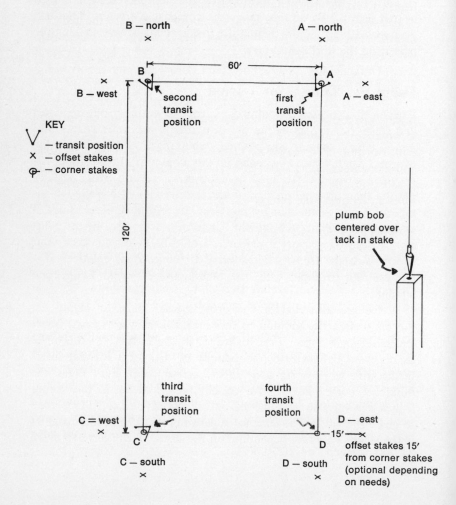

all your measurements from that precise point. Your objective is to set the transit over stake A, so that the plumb bob hangs precisely over the nail. You will need to practice this operation— and before you finish the court, you will have had lots of practice!

Facing the corner stake, set one leg of the tripod about two feet beyond the stake and pull the other two legs toward you, spreading them to either side of you, about two feet from the stake. (In order to level the base of the tripod, a leg on an uphill side of the stake will have to be set farther away. This will take experimentation.) Now the plumb bob should be hung from the transit and steadied, so that you can tell which way you must move the transit to center it exactly over the nail.

In adjusting the legs to bring the plumb bob over the nail, remember this simple rule: When you move a leg, the plumb bob will swing in the same direction (see Figure 21). By a series of patient adjustments, you will be able to bring the plumb bob within ½ inch of the nail.

The tripod base must be fairly level and the legs must be pressed firmly into the ground, so that the transit will not lose its position. It would be a miracle if you were able to position the tripod with only two moves; it may even take you a dozen tries the first time. But remember, if you are within ½ inch of the nail and if the base of the tripod is fairly level, the shifting plate and the leveling screws can finish the job.

Adjusting the Shifting Plate

Before using the shifting plate to position the plumb bob precisely over the nail, level the transit with the leveling screws. Otherwise, the final leveling procedure (which follows the plate adjustment) may move the plumb bob.

Now loosen two adjacent leveling screws (see Figure 22) enough so that you can slide the whole upper transit around on the shifting plate until the plumb bob is hanging directly over the nail. It is sometimes difficult to get the plumb bob to hang absolutely still. Stop it with your hand as well as you can. You will probably find it describing a tiny circle, but by watching carefully, you can make your plate adjustments to put the nail at the center of the plumb bob's small orbit. Then go through the leveling process you have already learned (pages 50–51).

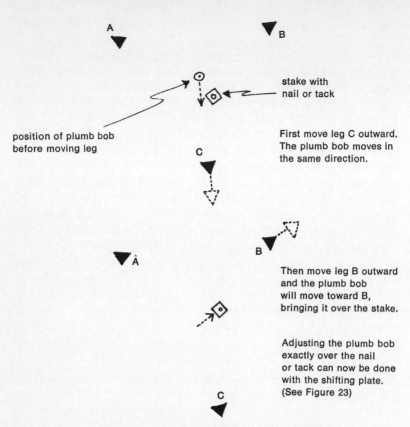

A

B

stake with
nail or tack

position of plumb bob
before moving leg

First move leg C outward.
The plumb bob moves in
the same direction.

C

B

A

Then move leg B outward
and the plumb bob
will move toward B,
bringing it over the stake.

Adjusting the plumb bob
exactly over the nail
or tack can now be done
with the shifting plate.
(See Figure 23)

C

FIGURE 21. Centering plumb bob over stake by moving legs

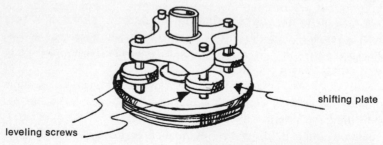

shifting plate

leveling screws

FIGURE 22.
Using shifting plate
to adjust bob over rail

Free (loosen slightly) any two adjacent
leveling screws so that the upper transit
can be slid about on the shifting plate.
When plumb bob is over nail,
gently tighten the leveling screws,
checking transit levels as you do.

Shooting the Stakes

As you can see in Figure 20, you can locate the position for six additional stakes from the first transit position. Aiming north, you can establish offset stake A-north. The distance is established by your helper, who uses a steel tape to measure fifteen feet (or your chosen distance from the actual boundary) in a northerly direction from corner stake A. You can tilt the telescope down and focus on the fifteen-foot mark on the tape, guiding your helper left and right. Your helper then drives a stake as close to position as possible. Next he checks with the tape again as you guide him with the telescope and he positions the stake, if it needs adjustment. Finally he drives a tack into the top of the stake to mark the exact offset point.

Now locate corner stake B and offset stake B-west. (You don't have to follow this order. I do it for illustration only. You can next do D and D-south if you prefer.) Loosen the upper clamp screw so that you can swing the telescope. Watching the scale, swing to the west to 270 degrees (one scale will read 90 degrees). Tighten the upper clamp screw and adjust exactly to 270 degrees with the upper tangent screw, using your magnifying glass.

(*Note:* Make a quick check of your levels and adjust if necessary.) Your helper can now run a tape sixty feet west, and you can guide him in placing corner stake B, using the cross hairs in the telescope. When the stake is in, have him drive a nail into the stake for the precise placement of the corner. Now place stake and tack fifteen feet beyond for offset stake B-west.

Now swing the telescope south, to 180 degrees, have your helper measure 120 feet, and place corner stake D and offset stake D-south by the same method.

"Dumping" the Transit

Surveyors use this technique because it saves time. If your transit is capable of dumping, I would suggest you use this maneuver. However, if it confuses you, ignore it.

Dumping means to turn the telescope head over heels, as in Figure 23, which allows you to make a quick sighting 180 degrees from your last one. Thus, you could have dumped the scope after

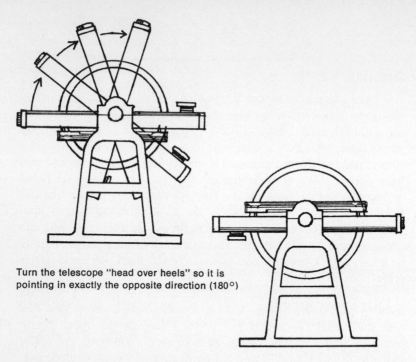

Turn the telescope "head over heels" so it is
pointing in exactly the opposite direction (180°)

FIGURE 23. "Dumping" the transit

your initial placement of A-north and placed D and D-south without loosening the upper motion or setting the vernier. Also, after
sighting B and B-west, you could have dumped the scope to place
A-east. In any case, before moving the transit, be sure you have
located A-east, either by dumping or by swinging the telescope
to 90 degrees (to the east).

Your chart should now indicate that you have placed seven
stakes including A, out of the twelve you need.

Moving the Transit

To place the remaining corner stake and four remaining offset
stakes, you must move the transit first to corner stake B and then
to corner stake C. Before lifting the transit, make sure to tighten
all three clamp screws, positioning the telescope as shown in Figure 24. Either remove the plumb bob or put it into your pocket
while still attached, fold the tripod legs, and carry the transit in

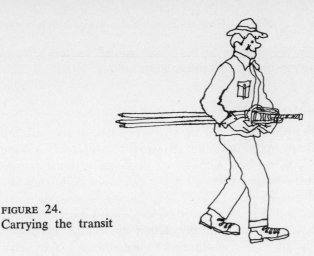

FIGURE 24.
Carrying the transit

your arms with the transit itself leading and the tripod legs behind. Be careful *never* to bump the instrument.

From corner stake B, you can shoot corner stake C, offset stake C-south, and then—by dumping the transit—offset stake B-north. From corner stake C you can set the two remaining offset stakes: C-west and D-east.

One caution: when you set up the transit on corner stake B, focus your cross hairs on corner stake A and set your scale exactly to the 90 degree mark. When you set up on corner stake C, focus your cross hairs on corner stake B and set your scale exactly to 0 degrees. This will assure you that your angles will be true and your court layout a perfect rectangle.

At times during the construction you may have to reset points that are lost because of the movement of material or machines—or just because of an accident. You will be able to reestablish any points by working from either corner stakes or any of the offset stakes.

Be sure to note on your grid chart the exact distance of each offset stake from its corner stake. This will be helpful in any resetting of stakes.

Using the Transit for Flatness and Grade

The transit will be used almost daily during construction to guide the work of leveling earth, grading, and laying down successive layers of material.

When using the instrument for ascertaining relative ground levels, you will need a rod and someone to hold it.

The Home-Made Rod

The rod used by professional surveyors is a pole that is marked off in feet and hundredths of a foot. However, because you and the people you will be working with are no doubt more familiar with feet and inches, I suggest that you make your own rod, using the standard ruler gradations.

To construct your rod, buy a good eight- or ten-foot steel tape—the kind that rolls up automatically. Using tiny nails, fasten it to an eight-foot length of one-by-three-inch pine; the end of the tape should be flush with the end of the pine board (see Figure 25). It's worth the investment to have a tape that is clearly and exactly

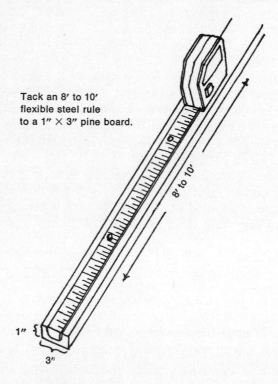

Tack an 8' to 10'
flexible steel rule
to a 1" × 3" pine board.

8' to 10'

1"

3"

FIGURE 25. Home-made rod

marked. When the court is complete, you can pull out the nails and the tape will be perfectly usable.

Working Method

The reading of levels (high and low points on the court) that you get from the transit and note on the grid chart will be your working guide from the first bulldozing operation to the final basecoat. At each stage you'll check the whole grid for comparative levels and note each grid-point level on the grid chart. It may seem arduous, and it will take time, but it is the only certain way to attain the ultimate goal—a flat playing surface, with the perfect grade for drainage.

Since you will be changing the level of the court area from day to day as you remove earth or add material, you should establish norms from which you can measure your ideal levels for each part of the area and for each layer of material.

Position the transit outside the court area, preferably on the low side, where the instrument can be placed each day without interfering with the movement of the bulldozer or the work crew. Drive a stake into the ground below the transit, letting it project a few inches above the ground, so that you can find it easily each day. This is the off-court transit position.

From here direct the "rod person" to each grid point in turn. Carefully sight the telescope on the rod so that you can read the ruler at the point where it is bisected by the horizontal cross hair. Using a pencil, write down the inches at each grid point on the grid chart.

Look at Figure 26 as an example. The figure shows sightings on just four grid points. You will actually take them over the entire court area. Let us suppose that you get the following readings: A-2 reads fifty-two inches; C-4 reads fifty-four inches; G-4 reads thirty inches; E-9 reads forty-one inches.

For the purposes of the example we will assume that A-2 is at the height we desire for it. In order to achieve a grade of one inch in every ten feet, we must make the grid points along line B one inch higher * than those along line A, those on line C one inch higher than those along line B, and so on.

---

* You will notice that you get *lower* readings on higher points because the rod is lifted in relation to the telescope level.

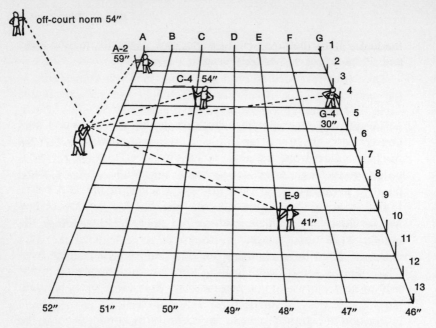

FIGURE 26. Sighting from an off-court transit position

Therefore, using A-2 as our norm, C-4 *should* read fifty inches when we have finished grading the earth or subbase. Thus, C-4 will need four inches of fill to bring it up to proper grade. Similarly, G-4 should read forty-six inches; so we will have to remove sixteen inches of earth and/or stone to achieve proper grade. Point E-9 should read forty-eight inches. Therefore, seven inches of earth must be removed.

As you take these readings and calculate the inches above or below proper grade for each grid point, note the plus or minus distance at each point on the grid chart. *Plus* indicates *above* proper grade; *minus* indicates *below*. In other words, next to C-4 write −4; at G-4 write +16; at E-9 write +7; and at A-2 put a check mark, indicating that it is correct.

This system of noting relative heights will be used during all stages of the work.

Resetting the Transit

When you have finished using the transit at the end of the day it must be taken indoors. The next day you use it, set it up over the stake at your off-court transit position, adjusting it to a comfortable working height and level it carefully.

Take your first reading on a grid point that you know to be at the correct level. In all likelihood, *you will not get exactly the same reading you got on the previous day of work.* In other words, when you sight on A-2, the reading may be more or less than fifty-two inches. This is because it is extremely difficult to set up the transit so that the telescope is exactly the same distance above ground twice in a row. Since we are dealing with *relative* heights, it is not necessary to get the same reading each day.

For example, if on the second day the reading at A-2 is 52½ inches, then that is the norm against which other sightings are judged. Thus, since on the previous day we calculated that G-4 should read 46 inches at ideal grade, it should now read 46½ to allow for the reset transit position.

You will find, working from day to day, that the only notations you will need on the grid chart are pluses, minuses, and check marks. This gives you the relative heights you want to achieve. As long as you know of *one* grid point that is correct, any of the others can be judged in relation to it.

Adding Layers of Material

Before adding new layers of material, it is important that you set up the transit and take a reading at a grid point you know to be at correct grade level. You will then have a standard by which to judge the desired level of each added layer of material. For instance, if your level at A-2 is 52½ inches and you are to add 4 inches of crushed rock, A-2 should read 48½ inches after the rock has been dumped and leveled. You will then have a standard for judging the relative levels you want to achieve over the whole court area with the new layer of material.

Off-Court Norm (optional)

As a permanent reference throughout the building process, you can establish an off-court norm—a position for the rod which will be unaffected by any of the construction work—and relate this norm to an on-court norm, such as we designated A-2 in Figure 27. Suppose, for example, that when our first reading at

A-2 was 52 inches the off-court-norm position gave us a reading of 54 inches. We could then take a reading on the off-court norm on any day and at any stage of the construction and have a relative height reference for comparison with any on-court position.

The off-court norm could be a flat rock or a stake driven into the earth. Whatever it is, note it on your grid chart so that you will not forget it.

Caution

It is a good practice to check the bubble level on the telescope as you swing from one grid point to another. It only takes a fraction of a second to glance at the bubble and be sure it is holding its position, and this simple precaution can make the difference between an accurate reading and one that will throw you off completely.

Another word of warning: as you begin work on the court each day, get into the habit of carrying the transit down to the work site and setting it up before you begin. Have a waterproof cover handy, in case of a shower. But don't use plastic in the hot sun; it may make the glass sweat. A white cloth is the best protection from sunlight.

You will quickly come to regard the transit as a valuable friend and ally on the job. You may even feel lonely if it isn't there beside you, ready to tell you that you're doing fine.

 DIESEL FUEL AND COLD BEER

We were having cocktails down the road with our friends the Clarks, and Dick wanted my wife, Nancy, and me to see the excavation they were doing for a new wing. That the Clarks needed a new wing was obvious when we saw Susannah come around the corner of the house to join us in the tour. Theirs was a growing family.

We all stared down at the cut on the north end of the house. The earth had been neatly removed to a depth of six or seven feet and piled at the east end of the cut. It had taken great skill with a bulldozer to work around some favorite trees, the house, and an old stone well that was to be preserved.

"You should have seen the guy," Dick said. "He handled it like a surgeon. No waste motions, never touched anything, and the excavation is so precise, they could start pouring cement right now."

"Who is he?" I asked.

"John Fehsal. Lives near here. I heard about him from my contractor. He said nobody else could do it."

"I wonder how he'd like to work on a tennis court," I said out loud to no one in particular.

"On a *what*?" Dick asked. "You mean . . . ?" He put the whole thing together without further conversation. "I'll get his phone number for you," he said, starting for the front door.

That's how we heard about John. And when John came over to the house and I asked him if he could give me a flat cut within two inches of level at every point in the court area, he just looked at the lawn for a minute and then asked, "Don't you want to get a little closer? How about an inch and a half?"

"There's one thing I forgot to tell you," Dick said when I told him John was going to take on the job. "John will take care of the diesel fuel. That's what the bulldozer runs on. But not John."

"What does John run on?"

"Cold beer."

The fact is, a diesel engine puts out quite a lot of heat. Sitting on it for a couple of hours straight, on a hot August day, would dehydrate a watermelon. John *did* run on cold beer. He boiled away five or six cans manipulating that yellow monster, and some of the job *did* slip to the two-inch tolerance. But, most of it was within an inch. I wasn't about to complain.

5.

Preparing the Subbase
and Base

The flat, compacted earth, leveled to the correct grade, is called the subbase. Preparing it can either be a relatively simple task or a difficult, arduous one, depending on the area you have chosen for the court. Small trees, earth, and loose stones are easy to move. Large trees with deep root systems may require heavy machinery. Rock ledges are best avoided if possible because they are very difficult to deal with.

Earth-Moving Machinery

To begin the job, you will need someone to operate a bulldozer, a bucket-loader, and possibly a ditchdigger. Choosing the person can best be accomplished by asking friends or neighbors who have used someone in the neighborhood. Or if you or a neighbor have used a builder, he may be able to recommend a good man for the job.

Most such men have several machines available to them; so you will not have to search for more than one good operator. He will have other drivers who assist him. Your objective is to find a skillful man whose prices are competitive in your area and who seems interested in doing a good job for you. Leveling to the tolerances you require demands patience and painstaking work with a bulldozer.

Ask your best prospects to look over the job with you, discuss how they would approach it, and quote their price by the hour or by the day—or both. (A well-operated bulldozer can accomplish an enormous amount of work in an hour.)

Assembling the other tools and the work force is a simple matter.

Tools and Equipment

YOUR OWN
  Rod
  Transit
  Grid chart
  Stakes, 1 x 2-inch pine, 15 to 18 inches long (44)
  Shovels, long and short handled
  Picks
  Mattocks
  Metal hand rakes
  Sledge hammer, 12 to 16 pound
  8-inch tamper
  Crowbar

TO BE RENTED (AS NEEDED)
  Bulldozer
  Bucket-loader
  Ditchdigger
  Trucks
  Motor rollers
    1,000 pound
    500 pound
  Dynamite (if needed)

Time

  Rough-grading
    2 to 5 days, clearing
    1 day, leveling

Drainage
  2 days for nonporous courts
  4 days for porous courts
Rock base
  10 to 15 days
Compaction
  1 day

Work Force

PROFESSIONAL
  Bulldozer and bucket-loader operator
  Ditchdigger operator
  Road-scraper operator (if you use one)
  Truckdriver (to deliver stone)
  Truckdriver (to move earth if needed)
  Blasting expert (if needed)

YOU, YOUR FAMILY, AND FRIENDS
  You
  2 or 3 helpers

Clearing the Ground

You will have to be prepared to be flexible in your approach to clearing the ground and rough-grading the court area. If you run into unexpected rock ledges or outcroppings, you may have to shift the position of the court or change its orientation slightly to avoid a large blasting job. If you are cutting into a hillside or dealing with a slope, it is sometimes hard to anticipate how much rock you will run into. Your bulldozer operator can help you here. Experienced operators have learned a great deal about what to expect under the earth's surface, especially if they have lived and worked in your area for many years.

You can probe for rock ledges by driving a crowbar down through the ground to the depth you hope to obtain. Do it gradually, widening the hole every few inches to make a small hole two to three feet deep, perhaps deeper, depending on your strength and the softness of the earth.

You can save money if before calling in the heavy machinery, you and your amateur helpers—strong ones—dig up bushes, cut down trees, and dig out all roots you can handle manually. Big trees with big root systems can be dug out with the bucket-loader or bulldozer. Do not leave any part of the root system. Remove *all* organic matter from the court area.

After the organic matter has been removed—and you must check this carefully—it would be a good idea to spray a strong weed killer on any area where there may be grass seed or other seeds.

Organic matter left in the ground can lead to disastrous problems. Seeds may germinate, and one day a small bush or tree or other plant may actually force its way up through the asphalt. On the other hand, organic matter that rots will disintegrate and leave a hollow area under the court, and this may eventually result in a depression in the court surface.

Blasting

If you encounter a rock ledge or large outcropping that encroaches on the area where the court *must* be and that cannot be moved by the bulldozer, find yourself an expert in the use of dynamite. Your bulldozer operator may be able to help with this search.

Filling

If you have an area that needs a great deal of fill—perhaps one corner of the court area drops off by several feet—you should first put in a rock base before you fill it with dirt. If you fill such an area with dirt alone—even though you compact it—it will eventually settle more than other areas of the court and cause a deep depression.

First dump large stone in the low area and then, after compacting the stone thoroughly with the weight of a bulldozer, build up the top foot or two with earth, six inches at a time, wetting and rolling each layer thoroughly.

Remember, what you are trying to achieve is the same degree of compaction that exists under areas of the court where the earth has settled for decades.

Rough Grading

Once you have cleared the ground in the court area and filled and compacted any obvious low points, you should set up the transit and with a helper working the rod and the grid chart at your side, check the levels over the whole court area (as discussed on pages 63–64). Then show the bulldozer operator what earth he will have to move to work toward the desired plane.

Don't forget that the materials you are going to use to make the court will raise the final level. Therefore, the earth level you want to achieve at this stage must allow for subsequent additions. You must decide in advance on the thickness of the court you are building and its eventual height in relation to the adjoining ground (for examples, see Figure 27).

The playing surface of the porous court will be five or six inches above the earth subbase. The playing surface of the non-porous court will be eleven or twelve inches above the subbase.

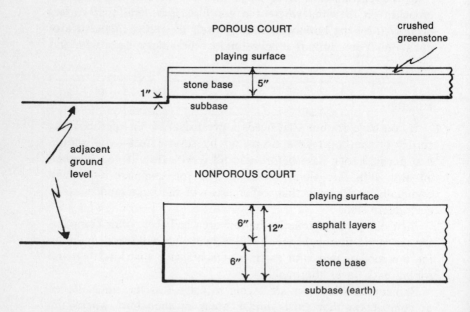

FIGURE 27. Levels of the porous and the nonporous court

Plan ahead. You can prevent surrounding ground water from running onto the court and improve drainage by making your finished court five or six inches higher than the area around it.

Drainage

Here again I must stress that your tennis court is in motion in relation to the world around it. The most significant movement is water, from above and from below. If you live in an area where the temperature drops below freezing, the effects of water are compounded.

If possible, study the court area and the surrounding terrain during a heavy rainfall, to see how quickly water drains and how well the ground seems to absorb it in the wet months of the year. If you are building in an area that does not drain, you will have to create drainage (as shown in Figure 28). A network of ditches with porous drainpipes and gravel surrounding the pipes will carry the water away from the court area.

If drainage is relatively good in and around the court area, a more modest drainage system will suffice (see Figure 29). Remember that it is better to err on the side of caution; more drainage is safer than less. It involves more work, more materials, and

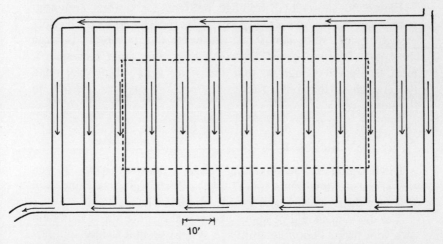

10'

FIGURE 28. Drainage for area that drains very poorly—porous court only. Drainage ditch and pipe every 10'

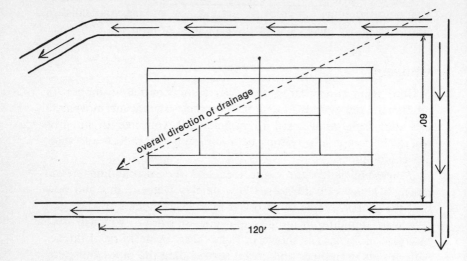

FIGURE 29. Average drainage system—porous or nonporous court

more time, but once the court is built, poor drainage is a serious fault that cannot easily be corrected.

Figure 30 shows two drainage patterns for porous and non-porous courts. As you already know, the porous court needs only a slight grade, since almost all the water drains rapidly through the court. The nonporous court is a huge, flat, solid rectangle; it must be tipped enough so that the water runs off quickly—and flat enough so that only a few, very shallow puddles are left on it after a rain.

Drainage Ditches

Ditchdigging is back-breaking work if done by hand. If you can afford the few hours it will take a ditchdigging machine, you will save days of work and avoid countless blisters.

The ditching should be about twelve inches wide and a minimum of a foot deep. Plan your drainage system so that it has approximately the same grade as a nonporous court (one inch in every ten feet). The grade can of course be steeper than this—but not shallower.

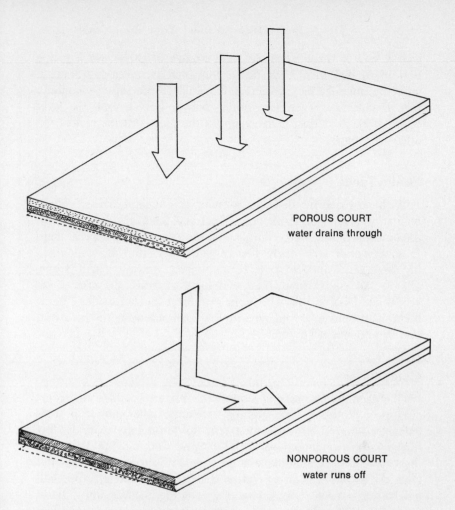

POROUS COURT
water drains through

NONPOROUS COURT
water runs off

FIGURE 30. Drainage patterns. Water drains *through* porous court.
Water runs *off* nonporous court.

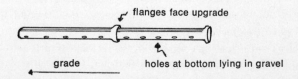

flanges face upgrade

grade

holes at bottom lying in gravel

FIGURE 31. Proper way to lay a drainpipe

Lay two or three inches of small stones or large gravel in the bottom of the ditch; then lay a four-inch perforated drainpipe, with the holes at the bottom and the flanges facing the upgrade (see Figure 31). Then add more stone or gravel, until the level of the stone is at least halfway up on the pipe. Fill the rest of the ditch with earth.

Drain Field

With an extensive drainage system, you must provide a drain field so that the water will not collect and back up into the court area, defeating the whole purpose of the drainage system. If there is no downhill area where the system can drain, you can dig a big drain pit, from 500 to 1,000 cubic feet, and fill it with stone, gravel, and coarse sand. You will have to judge the size of pit you need. Discuss this with your bulldozer–bucket-loader operator(s). Of course, if you have a low area adjacent to the court, you should not need a pit at all.

Compaction

Compacting, or pressing down, the material under the court area is a procedure that greatly accelerates the natural process called settling. Earth and stone tend to settle into spaces below them. When we loosen earth by digging and moving it, as we must to achieve our flat plane, a great deal of settling will gradually take place—more in areas where the earth is loosest, more still where it has been loosened to a greater depth. We must therefore pack the earth down, or *compact* it, to the same depth and to the same degree throughout the entire area beneath the court. Otherwise, natural settling will occur unevenly. Some slight settling will occur over the years, no matter how carefully we compact, but the closer you come to a perfectly even compaction under the entire court area, the better the chance that you will not develop depressed areas.

Most specifications for the building of a tennis court advise that while filling an area you water it down thoroughly and roll it with a 1,000-pound roller to optimum compaction after every six-inch addition. The United States Tennis Court and Track Builders

Association defines *optimum compaction* as "95 percent standard density at optimum moisture in accordance with ASTM D698." You probably don't know what that means, any more than I did when I first read it. But if you wet down each six-inch layer of fill—*thoroughly*—and compact it with a 1,000-pound motor roller, you will be achieving sufficient compaction.

If there is a solid rock ledge under one area of the court, it will have a density that you cannot possibly equal in other areas, no matter how well you compact the earth. For this reason, avoid laying the court directly on a rock ledge unless the ledge is covered by at least eighteen inches of earth. If you *can't* avoid this problem, I advise spending extra money on the rock base, which I discuss later in the chapter.

Earlier, when discussing rough grading, I said that you should use stone to fill any significantly low area. This bears repeating here. If you must fill an area more than two feet deep, put the stones in first. It can be any kind of stone available—tailings from a sand pit, broken-up cement from an old foundation, a dismantled stone wall, or large gravel if nothing else is available (although this is the most expensive way to do it). The stone itself should be compacted or settled thoroughly by running the bulldozer back and forth over it before putting on the layers of earth. A big caterpillar-track bulldozer can provide good, although rough, compaction.

Retaining Walls

The rock and earth fill should be carried at least eight or ten feet beyond the court area and fully compacted to ensure against gradual sliding of the material supporting the court. And if the ground falls away sharply at that point, it may be necessary to put in a retaining wall (see Figure 32). The wall can be made of stone, brick, cinder block, or cement block.

One kind of retaining wall is a *dry wall,* which has no cement or mortar between the stones. Building with fieldstone takes considerable skill because you must choose and arrange the stones so that they will hold their position firmly when laid one on top of the other. You may have to chip or break some of them with a mason's hammer to make them fit securely. However, when

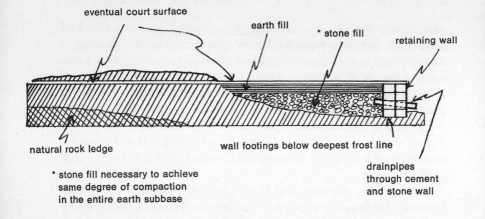

eventual court surface

earth fill

* stone fill

retaining wall

natural rock ledge

wall footings below deepest frost line

* stone fill necessary to achieve
same degree of compaction
in the entire earth subbase

drainpipes
through cement
and stone wall

FIGURE 32. Cross section of court built in sloping ground

laid properly, the interlocking stones produce a very firm and extremely handsome wall. And because there are air spaces between them, water can drain through freely. Thus, the dry wall is not itself affected by frost. Of course, the wall *is* somewhat affected by the heaving of the frozen, water-soaked earth next to it.

A wall using mortar or cement is far easier for the layman to construct. It may not be as attractive if you have too much cement showing, but if you install drainpipes here and there, water can drain away and the wall should survive many years of freezing and thawing. The pipes should go through the wall, near the base, so that water will not back up behind it. To escape heaving by frost in northern latitudes, set the base of the wall on footings that go below heavy frost level. This could be as little as twelve inches or as much as three feet.

The Rock Base

The layer of rock in the base of the court serves three purposes: stability, drainage, and frost-protection. The sheer weight and mass of four to six inches of heavy crushed rock provides firmness under the court, which is an invaluable protection against settling or shifting. Since water can run through it freely without moving it, the rock base aids drainage of the porous court and nonporous court alike. And finally, this base keeps water from forming puddles and freezing under the court surface, which can cause heaving of the layers above.

After the earth subbase has been thoroughly compacted and it is within one inch of the desired flat plane at all points, you are ready to put down the crushed rock.

For the porous court the rock base consists of a four-inch layer of ¾-inch stone topped by a one-inch layer of screenings, or stone dust.

The nonporous court (see Figure 33) requires an underlying layer of the heaviest crushed rock, which is used in building the super highways. The pieces of rock average 1½ inches and the layer should be four inches deep in most areas where there is frost.

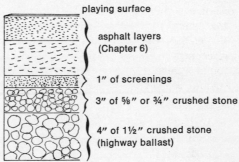

playing surface

asphalt layers
(Chapter 6)

1″ of screenings

3″ of ⅝″ or ¾″ crushed stone

4″ of 1½″ crushed stone
(highway ballast)

FIGURE 33.
Layers of the nonporous court

The extra layer of 1½-inch stone is very important. The added weight helps to make the court mass inert and thus more rigid. And the nonporous court depends on almost perfect rigidity to maintain its flatness year after year. This layer should be topped by a three-inch layer of ¾-inch or ⅝-inch stone, and this in turn by a one-inch layer of screenings. However, the depth of the layers should vary in accordance with the lowest average winter temperature. This will avoid paying for more material than is necessary in warmer climates and will minimize the effects of deeper frosts in colder climates. The following table gives some general guidelines for both porous and nonporous courts.

DEPTH OF MATERIALS (Before compaction)

Lowest average winter temperatures

Fahrenheit	32° and above	20° to −10°	−10° to −20°	−30° and below
Celsius	0° and above	−6.6° to −23°	−23° to −29°	−35° and below

POROUS COURTS				
1½″ stone	none	none	3″	4″
¾″ stone	4″	4″	4″	5″
screenings	1″	1″	1″	1″
NONPOROUS COURTS				
1½″ stone	3″	4″	5″	6″
¾″ or ⅝″ stone	1½″	3″	4″	5″
screenings	1″	1″	1″	1″
rough asphalt	3″	3½″	4″	4″
smooth asphalt	2″	2½″	3″	4″

Quantity of Materials

Depending on the depth of the materials you use, based on the Table on page 79, it is easy to calculate the quantity you will need for each layer. For a court that is a full 120 by 60 feet, it will take approximately 22.2 yards of material for each one inch of depth. Since crushed stone weighs approximately 1.4 tons per yard, you will need approximately 31.1 tons of crushed stone for 1 inch of depth. If the court area is not standard, then follow this formula: length of court (in inches) times width of court (in inches) divided by 46656 (number of cubic inches in a cubic yard) equals the number of cubic yards for each one inch of material.

The following table will guide you in ordering crushed stone for a standard 120 by 60 foot court:

Depth in inches when spread	Cubic yards	Tons	Depth in inches after compacting
1	22.22 ∞	31	½
1½	33.33 ∞	47	1
2	44.44 ∞	62	1½
2½	55.55 ∞	78	2
3	66.66 ∞	93	2½
3½	77.77 ∞	109	3
4	88.88 ∞	125	3½
5	111.11 ∞	156	4½
6	133.33 ∞	187	5½

Laying the Rock Base (nonporous courts)

The techniques for laying the crushed stone for the porous and nonporous court are quite different. Therefore, the remainder of this chapter will deal with the nonporous court only. The laying of the rock base for the porous court will be explained in Chapter 7.

One-and-a-Half-Inch Stone

For this job you need a truckdriver who will lay the stone from his dump truck with great care and patience. It is extremely difficult to move heavy crushed stone by hand. That, of course, is one of its virtues. But you'll have a hard time respreading it once it is laid. This means that before you start, you and the driver will have to agree on the total amount of stone and on the thickness you are striving for. Then he should back to the end of the court, raise the truck body, and drive forward slowly, raising the body a little at a time, to allow the truck to put down the stone in as close to the desired thickness as possible. As the truck proceeds along the court, you will have to judge whether you're using too much or too little stone and signal the driver accordingly.

When he has finished you will need the bulldozer to finish the spreading. Nail a stick under your rod before checking the levels (see Figure 34). Otherwise, the rod will slip down between the

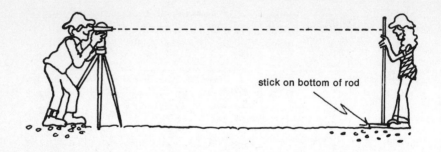

stick on bottom of rod

FIGURE 34. When using the transit on a rough surface, fasten a stick to the bottom of the rod, so it will not slip down into hollows or crevices.

large pieces of the stone layer. The stick will raise the rod slightly, but since we are interested in relative heights, this is of no concern. Completely check the grid and fill in your grid chart.

If there is still a great deal of stone to be moved to achieve the desired plane, you may want the bulldozer to do some more work. If not, you can do it by hand. You'll need your strongest workers, using cultivators and rakes. The long tines of cultivators move the heavy stone more readily. When your largest errors over the whole court area are one inch, compact the stone with a 1,000-pound roller. If you are afraid to attempt the rolling yourself, ask your bulldozer operator if he can do it or if he can suggest someone equipped to do it.

The Middle Layer

This layer can be of ⅝- or ¾-inch stone, depending on what is available locally. The procedure for laying it is similar to the one used for the 1½-inch stone, except that you will not need the bulldozer for spreading, since this stone is much easier to move by hand.

When the truck has spread the stone as evenly as possible, use shovels, wheelbarrows, and hand rakes to level this layer. Check the whole grid with the transit and rod and then carefully finish leveling. You may have to make several transit checks, and the leveling may take many hours of work. If there are high areas, take off the excess and spread the stone to low ones. If there are large low areas left even after leveling the high ones, dump more rock, to fill.

Be patient. Get within ½ inch of the desired plane. Again, compact the stone with a 1,000-pound roller, and if you have any doubts of having achieved your plane, recheck with the transit. If you find errors of more than 1 inch, correct them and roll the area again. If the error is between ½ inch and 1 inch, it can be corrected by the final layer.

Screenings

Also called stone dust, this is the smallest product of stone crushing which is left from the crushing operation. Much of it has the consistency of sand. It is very easy to move around and thus makes an easy layer to bring into a very precise plane. When you have finished raking this layer, it should be within ¼ inch of the desired plane. Now you are ready for compaction. Roll the entire court thoroughly.

It is vital to achieve an almost perfect plane before laying the asphalt. Make a careful check of the entire grid, using the transit and rod and marking your chart at each grid point. You must adjust the screenings and roll them once more if you've slipped beyond the ¼-inch tolerance.

This all takes time and patience, but the more accurate you are at this stage, the better the chance that the asphalt will achieve a nearly perfect plane. Bear in mind that the asphalt spreader will follow the level of the screenings and its wheels will, to some extent, also follow any imperfections.

BERMUDA SHORTS AND TRAP ROCK

When it came time to order crushed stone, I dutifully opened the Yellow Pages and called the New York Trap Rock Company, which informed me that if I were building a new thruway, they might be interested but that for one tennis court, I would have to find an independent supplier. When I asked for suggestions, they had only one: Storms Trucking.

Storms Trucking turned out to be a homey-sounding woman who listened to my story and then turned me over to a gentleman named Ted Brubaker.

I told Ted what I had in mind. We discussed the size of stone for the first layer and some other details, like cost, and he said he'd be over in the morning.

At 8:30 the next morning, exactly on time, a huge ten-wheel truck rumbled up in front of the house and stopped with a hiss of air brakes. I hurtled out of the house to lead the monster toward the court area. When it reached the site, it again hissed and grunted to a stop.

A slim, soft-spoken man, wearing Bermuda shorts and loafers, stepped down lightly from the cab and put out his hand. "Mr. Anderson, I'm Ted Brubaker." The accent sounded more like Princeton than the Teamsters' Union.

I had to adjust my expectations. I had gone all the way from one of the largest rock suppliers in the country to a one-truck, one-family operation—and obviously, a very unusual family in the world of heavy trucking.

I described what I wanted Ted to do with the rock—to let it out gradually in rows approximately four inches deep. "I know it can't be done that accurately," I said, "but I just want you to know what the objective is, so you can come as close as possible."

"No problem," he told me. "I've done it before."

"Tennis courts?"

"One," he said. "Down in Tappan, several years ago."

"Not Don Ackerson!"

"That's the fellow," said Ted. "Worked out pretty well."

He hitched up his Bermuda shorts, made the long step up into the truck, and I stopped worrying.

6.

The Nonporous Court

You are about to be the owner of the largest parking lot in your neighborhood. At least, that's what it looks like when the asphalt has been laid and rolled. But when the net is up and the lines are painted, it will become a magic place.

Correct installation of the asphalt layers is critical because once laid it is virtually impossible to change them. They can only be corrected by adding material on top. The flatness and stability of the finished court depend on the flatness and even compaction of the two layers of asphalt—the rough underlayer (or binder course) and the finer grained upper layer.

The most satisfactory asphalt application is the hot, plant-mixed type which is used in building driveways and parking lots. When properly installed, it will form a virtually permanent base for your court. Although it is possible for amateurs to work with what is called jobmix asphalt, this is a less satisfactory material and installation is an enormous amount of work. Assuming that you use the former type, the job will require dump trucks, a source of hot asphalt reasonably close to the site—that is, within a thirty-minute drive by truck—and a paving machine, with experts operating it.

In Chapter 2 I discussed briefly the task of finding a good

asphalt man. It bears further discussion right here. Gather recommendations from anyone and everyone—your bulldozer operator, your crushed rock supplier, and friends and neighbors who have had extensive driveway paving done. Discuss the job with the most promising prospects. Let them know that the goal is to lay the asphalt within ⅛ inch of the desired plane. But also let them know that you are going to help achieve that with careful transit work. Discuss costs per square foot or yard, so that you have some comparative prices. And as you have done with your other professionals, assess each candidate's eagerness to meet your requirements.

The ideal contractor has equipment especially designed for tennis court installation. If he has a computerized paving machine, which automatically seeks a preprogrammed level, he is capable of giving you an almost perfect job. However, it is more likely that you will have to work with a man who uses a standard driveway paving machine. In which case, you *and* he will have to work very slowly, carefully checking levels with great frequency.

In any event, you can't sit back and let the experts take over. While they're spreading the asphalt, you must employ your transit, rod, and grid chart to indicate the corrections that the first layer must achieve. Then when it is down and sufficiently hardened, you must determine what corrections must be made when the upper layer of asphalt is laid. Paint these corrections on the first asphalt layer at each grid point so the asphalt man can see them clearly when running the paving machine. There is no rest for the boss!

Installing the asphalt is the most expensive part of the job, but it is critical to the success of a stable nonporous court. If you cannot spend the money, then I strongly advise that you choose to build the fast-dry, porous court described in Chapter 7.

If you want to consider or reconsider the budgetary requirements for the nonporous court, turn to Appendix B. But before abandoning the nonporous court for financial reasons, read pages 94–96, which describe the grass-strip alternative. It offers a way of saving almost 25 percent of the rock and asphalt cost.

The Net-Post and Net-Strap Anchor Plugs

Before the asphalt is installed, I recommend that you construct two simple, wooden plugs (see Figure 35), which will displace

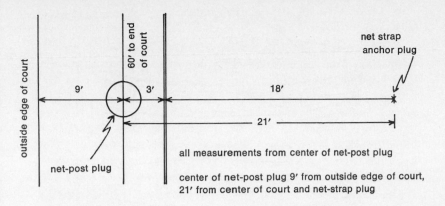

FIGURE 35. Locating position of net-post plug and net-strap anchor plug

the asphalt from the area the net posts and cement will later occupy. After the asphalt has been laid and rolled, the plugs are removed, leaving neat round spaces for the excavation of the net-post holes. Without the plugs, you would have to dig thirty-inch circles out of the asphalt. It can be done, but it is much harder work than building the plugs. Why risk a sore back or even worse, a case of tennis elbow?

You should also put a tennis-ball can or a can of similar size into the asphalt where the center-strap anchor is to be cemented. Again, this will be easier than digging away the asphalt.

Figure 35 indicates the positions for this plug and the net-post anchor plugs. *Your measurements must be accurate* because the placement of the net posts will eventually determine the position of the playing lines on the finished court.

Building the Net-Post Anchor Plugs

Time Schedule

1 or 2 days (depending on how good your equipment is for sawing the circles of plywood)

Work Force

You
1 helper (if available)

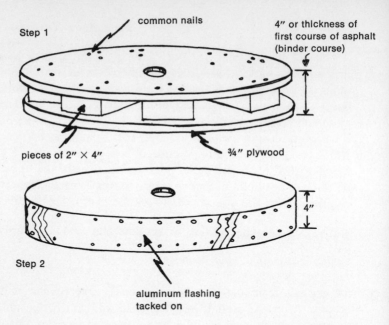

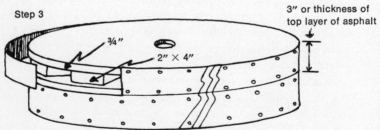

FIGURE 36. Construction of the net-post anchor plug

Tools and Materials

¾-inch plywood and ½-inch plywood, cheapest grade, circular, 30-inch diameter

Aluminum flashing

Short ends of two-by-four

Hammer, nails, tacks

Scraps of wood (optional, depending on desired thicknesses)

The plugs are built in two layers, as Figure 36 indicates. The first layer is built to the approximate thickness of the underlayer of asphalt, the second to the thickness of the upper layer.

Cut out two circular discs of ¾-inch plywood, each 30 inches in diameter. Make a sandwich, using pieces of two-by-four and other scraps of wood as needed for filler to make the whole sandwich as thick as the underlayer of asphalt is to be. Tack the aluminum flashing around the edge of the sandwich; this will make it easier to remove the plywood after the asphalt has hardened and will leave a smoother asphalt edge. When the first layer of asphalt has hardened for a few hours, you can then build the upper layer of the net-post plugs. Secure them to the bottom layer with a couple of nails and you are ready for the next layer of asphalt.

Laying the Asphalt

Tools, Equipment, and Materials

YOUR OWN
Transit
Rod
Grid chart
Small can of white paint and
2-inch brush
13-foot scaffolding boards (4)
Stakes
Ball of heavy cotton cord
Small sledge hammer (for stake-driving)

TO BE SUPPLIED BY YOUR ASPHALT MAN
Asphalt-paving machine (asphalt spreader)
Asphalt trucks (2 or 3)
Asphalt rakes, hoes, and tamper(s)
Motor rollers
  2,000 pounds
  1,000 pounds
89 yards asphalt, binder course (¾-inch stone)
67 yards asphalt, top course, ¼-inch stone (#17)

Work Force

PROFESSIONAL
3 men to lay asphalt
  1 man to operate paving machine
  2 men to rake, check levels, and smooth asphalt
  2 truckdrivers to bring asphalt

YOU, YOUR FAMILY, AND FRIENDS
You
1 helper to check levels with transit

Time

Rolling and patching the screenings: 1 day
Laying the first course of asphalt: 2 days (depending on distance of court from asphalt source)
Rolling the first course and checking the levels: 1 day
Curing the first course: 3 to 4 days
Laying the top asphalt course: 2 days
Rolling, checking: 1 day
Curing: in 3 to 4 days it can be walked on and lines may be applied for temporary use. Final playing surface should not be applied for at least 6 weeks to allow for complete curing.

Outlining the Asphalt Area

The asphalt man will need a clear outline of the area he is to cover. Although the rock base itself is an approximate guide, the rock is likely to spill over the sides a bit here and there, so that your boundaries will not be exact.

If you have not already driven the offset stakes into place for earlier work, you must do so now. The stakes must be solidly fixed and should protrude at least twelve inches above the ground, with strings pulled taut to indicate the outside limits of the asphalt (see Figure 37).

Laying the First Course of Asphalt

The asphalt man will use the string as an exact guide when he operates the paving machine.

The most efficient way to operate the machine is from one end of the court to the other. The trucks come one at a time back down the court, fill the paving-machine hopper with hot asphalt, and then go off to pick up another load. To lay the first course, the machine moves very slowly, depositing exactly the right depth of asphalt in an even strip. By the time the hopper is empty, the next truck should have arrived to reload it.

Using special rakes, hoes, and tampers, the professional crew

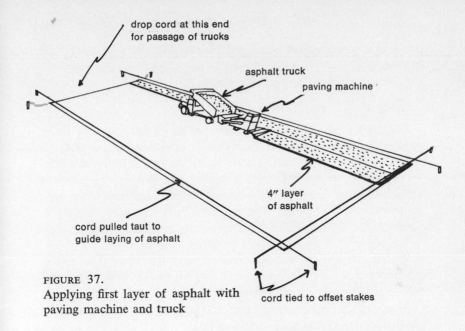

FIGURE 37.
Applying first layer of asphalt with
paving machine and truck

should smooth out any imperfections as each strip is completed. Likewise, they must go over the butting of the strips, so that it is exactly even and there is no ridge to mar the flatness of the plane. Bear in mind that the rolling will compress the whole surface by almost ½ inch and get rid of tiny flaws, while revealing larger ones, which must then be repaired with extra asphalt and a tamper.

Checking the First Course

When the first course has been laid and rolled, go immediately to work with the transit, rod, and grid chart. Make a careful check over the entire grid, mark the chart, and take a small paint brush and some white paint to *mark the readings on the asphalt itself*. Using a garden hose, flood the court, let it dry for about an hour, and outline the remaining puddles with white paint.

Patching

Any areas that are more than ½ inch lower than the desired plane should be patched with asphalt and rolled again. Recheck the patched areas, and if necessary to achieve the ½-inch tolerance, do some additional patching. Ideally, you should be within

¼ inch of the desired plane before starting the top course of asphalt.

Laying the Top Course of Asphalt

The paving machine tends to minimize flaws and eliminate small variations from the desired plane because it lays the asphalt in ten-foot strips, each of which will be precisely flat if the machine is operated properly. The critical area is the butting, or point at which the strips meet. When the edge of the machine rolls over an area that is either too high or low (and you have marked it clearly), the operator can adjust the depth of the asphalt he's depositing in that area and thus eliminate the problem.

If the patching of the first course was done carefully and if the application of the top course follows these principles, you should achieve an almost perfect plane.

In any case, further corrections will be possible when the playing surface is applied (see Chapter 12).

Curb Around the Asphalt

There are several ways of handling the finished edge of the asphalt. If your lawn is to meet the edge of the court, you can simply leave the asphalt very neatly beveled and tamped and then fill the earth in to meet it (see Figure 38A).

You don't have to worry about retention of the asphalt; it will hold this edge very well if it is tamped firmly and smoothly. If the edge is to be exposed, you can leave the beveled asphalt edge unprotected, or if the court is on a high slope, you may have to construct a retaining wall (see Figure 38B). It would be very unwise to leave the edge of the court exposed if it is next to an unsupported earth slope of any depth. The settling of the earth would probably cause the edge of the court to sink. You can achieve a very neat-looking edge by laying bricks flat, end to end, in a layer of cement, with cement between them (see Figure 38C).

The Curing of the Asphalt

When the asphalt job has been completed, ideally it should be allowed to cure for about six weeks before the playing surface

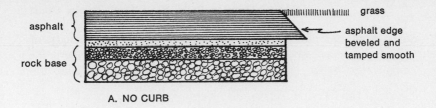

A. NO CURB

asphalt
rock base

grass
asphalt edge
beveled and
tamped smooth

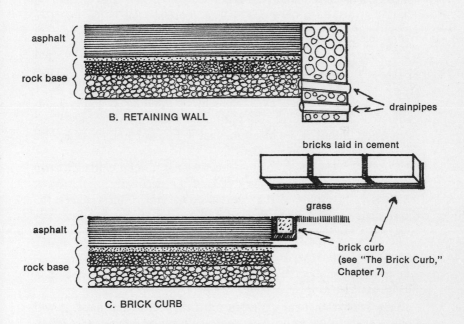

asphalt
rock base

B. RETAINING WALL

drainpipes

bricks laid in cement

grass

asphalt
rock base

C. BRICK CURB

brick curb
(see "The Brick Curb,"
Chapter 7)

FIGURE 38. Finishing the edge of the asphalt

is installed. There are volatile petroleum gases and solvents in the asphalt, and these must be allowed to escape. If you trap them with the playing surface, they will bubble through and partially—or even completely—destroy your surface. After three or four weeks, curing will be fairly well completed. However, the longer curing time is safer. If your schedule permits, let the asphalt sit over the winter and install the finished surface in the first warm spring weather. You can install fencing and net posts (see Chapters 8 and 9), put lines on the asphalt, and play on it in the meantime. Although it will wear your sneakers and tennis balls quickly, and stain them as well, you'll be playing *tennis* and the novelty of having the court should more than compensate for the slight inconvenience. Also, after playing on asphalt, you'll appreciate the playing surface even more when you have applied it.

The Grass-Strip Alternative

From my own experience, I recommend the grass-strip alternative wholeheartedly if your court is surrounded by lawn. It has some minor drawbacks but many more assets, as far as I'm concerned—and I think my wife and all our tennis-playing friends would agree most of the time.

Long before we had even thought of building a court, I encountered the grass strip on Gardner Botsford's court on Long Island and found it so pleasant that I remembered it when we started to plan our own court.

What is it? The grass strip is exactly what it sounds like: a strip of grass five feet wide, running around the perimeter of the court which is in fact part of the normal court area. This reduces the dimensions of the asphalt area to 110 feet by 50 feet but does not reduce the area available for play (see Figure 39).

Advantages of the Grass Strip

First, it is aesthetically pleasing. It helps blend the hard, paved surface of the nonporous court with the lawn or other landscaping. Second, the grass strip helps to prevent balls that roll onto the grass out of play from rolling back onto the court. For instance, when a first serve goes deep, you almost never have to stop to retrieve the ball.

Last, and certainly not least, grass is less expensive than asphalt. You save 1,700 square feet of asphalt, about 24.6 percent of the normal 7,200 square feet. If you are paying $.70 per square foot, that amounts to a saving of $1190.00. The grass seed needed for the strip will cost about $25.00 for the same area, and the rest —leveling, raking, and rolling—is your labor, which is free. You will also save the cost of 1,700 square feet worth of crushed stone; at $.185 per square foot, this amount to $315.00.

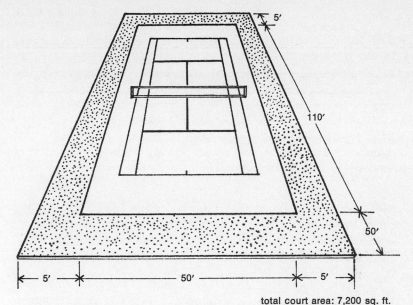

total court area: 7,200 sq. ft.
asphalt area: 5,500 sq. ft.
grass area: 1,700 sq. ft.
a saving of 1,700 sq. ft.
of crushed stone and asphalt

FIGURE 39. The grass-strip alternative

Disadvantages of the Grass Strip

First, the grass does not dry as quickly as the asphalt area after a rain, although you can lessen the problem if the grass is cut short and you run a Rol-Dri (see Appendix F) around on it. The sponge of the Rol-Dri removes the droplets from the blades or pushes them down to the base of the grass shoots, where they dampen the balls less. Second, the grass tends to be slippery when wet. And third, it requires more maintenance than asphalt. But assuming that you mow your lawn, anyway, the grass strip will not make much extra work for you.

Installation of the Grass Strip

Most of what you need to know is discussed in Chapter 10. You will want to plant a hardy grass that will stand up to the play and will be satisfactory even during the winter months, when the grass is dormant.

The area of the grass strip must be treated as carefully as the

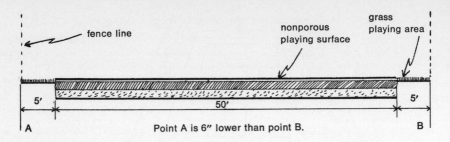

Point A is 6″ lower than point B.

FIGURE 40. The grass strip is graded exactly the same as the rest of the court (1 inch to 10 feet).

asphalt area in terms of leveling and compacting to the desired plane (see Figure 40). Compaction before seeding should be thorough enough so that the grass area will not sink after a few months. However, unlike the asphalt area, the grass strip can be corrected from time to time, whenever necessary.

If you do choose this alternative, complete the grass strip right after the asphalt; because it is important to get grass growing, so that the earth will not erode in the rain.

RAIN

The rollers kept going back and forth. The humming of the motors was constant, as Tony and his son rolled methodically—Tony, Sr., in one direction, Doug, in the other—back and forth to compact the material thoroughly and make it as hard and flat as possible. Tony's pipe sent up a thin stream of smoke behind him. And finally the pattern was complete. Each man had gone back and forth twice, completely covering the court on each circuit. The rollers followed each other off the court and onto the driveway, and both men climbed down. Tony knocked out his pipe on his shoe with two deft flicks of the wrist and stopped to look at the job. Some kind of crisis had been passed—a critical stage of work was now thoroughly completed.

Tony's face crinkled into a smile. "How does it look?"

"Damned good parking lot," I said. My face split with a grin. I shook his hand and then Doug's. We were all smiling.

"You got a damned good court there." Tony was proud of his work.

"I know it," I said.

The men started to get their gear into the pick-up truck. They ran one of the rollers onto the flat-bed. Tony said they'd come back for the other roller Monday morning, on their way to the next job.

I was moving some of the boards around, straightening up some of the construction debris that always accumulates, when Nancy came back from shopping.

"Have they finished?" she asked, wide-eyed. It had actually happened!

We stood there, looking at a big, flat expanse of asphalt—black, solid, and smooth—surrounded by raw, upturned earth. Beyond, lay the lawn on one side and the gently flowing, glistening brook on the other. The court was a real eyesore, come to think of it. Suppose it had been a parking lot? It would have been a hateful sight there, in the midst of the green. But somehow the asphalt was nothing short of beautiful because of its purpose: it was a tennis court!

I awoke with a start early the next morning. There was a sound, an ordinary enough one, of rain on the shingle roof. But it had a very special meaning for me that made me sit bolt upright and then, after a moment's thought, jump out of bed and rush to the window.

Nancy's voice was alarmed. "What's the matter?"

"It's raining," I said.

She just looked at me, as though to say, It has rained before and he hasn't acted this way.

"I mean it's raining on the *court*."

Now she was coming to. "Well, of course it is."

"And I think it's *running off,*" I said, feeling exultant. Nancy slid quickly out of bed and came to the window. We stood there, peering down through the branches, watching the water, which was making little rivulets from east to west. "I've got to go down there." I started to leave the window.

At that moment I saw someone turn into our neighbor's driveway, which passes the court. It was a pick-up truck. It stopped at the brow of the hill, and a stocky man climbed out, wearing a slicker and a beat-up fedora. He had a pipe clamped between his teeth. He stood for a moment and then walked along the brow of the hill to a point above the center of the court.

A minute later I hurried up to Tony and without speaking, stopped at his side.

He didn't turn, but he must have felt my eyes on his face. "Looks pretty good." Then he looked at me, and we were both grinning.

"There doesn't seem to be one place where it's making a puddle," I observed scientifically. "It's all running slowly off the court."

To Tony this did not seem miraculous. "Darned good thing," he said. "I'd hate to rip it up and start over."

We watched for a few more moments. I could feel some of the rain running off my hat brim and down inside my collar.

"How about a cup of coffee?"

"No, thanks. I've got to get to work." He put his hand out. It was a hard, muscular hand, with a little rain water on it. I tried to give back a good, friendly grip, but my hand felt insubstantial in his.

A moment later he had swung up into the truck and was backing out of the driveway. I returned to the house and climbed back into bed. Nancy was wide awake and excited. She could tell that everything was fine. It was written all over her face when she kissed me.

"It's all running off the court!"
"Darned good thing. I'd hate to rip it up and start over."

7.

The Porous Court

When I first played tennis, I had never heard of a *non*porous court. A tennis court was a flat place covered with clay, surrounded by a fence and painted with some lines. It had to be weeded in the corners where no one ran around much.

When I was about nine years old, our neighbors across the road built a court. They discovered quite a bit of clay in the subsoil once they scraped off the topsoil; so they called it a clay court. Their son was my age, and with the help of his father, he and I learned to play.

When I was in my early teens, our neighbors separated, and the court went to weeds. Tennis all but disappeared from my life for a while.

And then I made some new friends, who lived two miles down the road and had a court. They invited me to play. When I rode my bike down there and opened the gate to the court, I was dumbfounded. I'd never seen anything as beautiful, except the grass courts at Forest Hills.

There were several players sitting on the side, and there was a doubles match going on. Everyone was in whites, and the game looked very expert.

I asked an onlooker what they called the court.

"*En tout cas*," he replied.

I knew no more than I had before asking.

Later I found out that it meant "in all cases," or, in other words, in all weather. I didn't learn until many years later that the surface could more accurately have been described as crushed crystalline greenstone.

For many years I played on that court. Except for the rolling and brushing which we all had to share, it was a joyful experience, one I never tired of and one I'll never forget.

The virtues of the porous court are many: it does not fight nature and the forces of the environment, as does the hard court. It lets the water run through it. It bends and heaves with the earth, then settles back virtually unchanged. (Whereas the non-porous court survives only if it is strong enough to withstand the bending and heaving). The porous court is gentle on the feet and on the tennis balls. It slows the play and makes for longer rallies. It adds spice with the occasional imperfect bounce.

And it is less expensive to build.

The disadvantages have chiefly to do with maintenance. A porous court must be cared for almost daily during the playing season. And the season is relatively short in frost zones. On a non-porous court you can play all year—if it is not wet or covered with snow—but the porous court must "hibernate" in the very cold weather. It even has to be covered with a blanket, for protection from the worst effects of winter.

I like to be able to walk onto the court and start playing at any time of year, even if I have to wear gloves. But if you like the feel and the playing qualities of the fast-dry court enough to put up with the limitations, you can save two to three thousand dollars over the cost of the asphalt base court.

The big saving is in not having to hire an asphalt contractor. If you and your crew can put down the rock base properly, you will have no trouble putting down the crushed crystalline greenstone playing surface. If you want to pay a little extra for assurance that you are doing it properly, at least one big supplier of fast-dry material, who operates over wide areas of the eastern United States, will provide a supervisor for about ten days, to guide you in your work.

However, I see no need for this outside help if you follow the instructions carefully and work through the job step by step, without trying to break speed records. Although I suggest time schedules, never rush your work to keep up with a schedule. Do it right, not fast.

Look in Appendix A for information on suppliers of crushed crystalline greenstone, the most widely used fast-dry material.

And now to work.

Time

Dig sprinkler-system trench and drain pit
2 days
Install brick curbing
3 days
Prepare screed strips and straightedge
1 day
Install and level stakes and strips
2 days
Lay, level, and compact ¾-inch stone and screenings
2 to 3 days
Prepare and lay screed strips for fast-dry material
1 day
Lay, water, and compact fast-dry material
6 days (1 per row)

Work Force

PROFESSIONAL
Plumber (optional)

YOU, YOUR FAMILY, AND FRIENDS
You
3–5 strong helpers

Tools, Equipment, and Materials

Shovels (2)
Spade (2)
Picks (2)
Mattocks (2)

Metal hand rakes (4)
Hoe
Trowels (3)
Small sledge hammer (to drive grade stakes)
Mason's wheelbarrows with pneumatic tires (2 or 3)
Garden hose with good water supply
Transit
Rod
Grid chart
Motor rollers
  1,000-pound (rented)
  500- to 600-pound (purchased—you'll need one permanently,
    so it's a good idea to buy one now and save rental)
120 feet ¾-inch pipe
170 feet 1-inch pipe
1¼-inch pipe, enough to reach water source
Reciprocating sprinklers (5)
Elbows
Valves
Joints
Bricks, 8 by 3½ by 2¼ inches, common sand and cement (550)
Cement (8 or 9 bags)
1 yard of washed sand
Screed strips for stone, 1 inch by 4 inches by 12 to 16 feet
  840 running feet if you do not build curbs
  600 running feet if you install curbs
Straightedge, 2 inches by 10 inches by 12 feet
Angle irons, 24-foot to fasten to bottom of straightedge (see
    Figure 48)
Screws for angle irons
Stakes, 1 by 2 by 12 inches
Nails, 6-penny, 2-inch (6 pounds)
89 yards or 125 tons ¾-inch stone, (⅝-inch stone if more
    easily obtained)
12 yards or 16 tons (approximately) screenings
40 tons fast-dry surfacing material (crushed crystalline green-
    stone) (1,000 80-pound bags)
Screed strips for fast-dry material, 1¼ inches by 3 or 4 inches
    by 14 to 20 feet, 240 running feet
Tin strip, 12 inches wide, 10 to 12 feet long

Sprinkler System

Watering the court is an almost daily part of proper maintenance during the playing season. Nothing else will be as important as keeping the court moist. This is a tedious job when it is done with a garden hose. The hose itself tends to mess up the surface to some extent. It takes considerable time to set up portable sprinklers, wait for them to soak an area, then move them to the next area—and the next and the next. For this reason I recommend installing a sprinkler system. It will save you countless hours. Decide now. You'll have to do the job before laying the stone base for your court.

If you decide to put in a sprinkling system, I suggest that you hire a good plumber unless you pride yourself on your plumbing or someone in your work force does. But you will have to provide the plumber with the information about what you want to achieve. And of course, before the plumber comes, you should dig the ditches yourself, to minimize the time he needs to spend at twelve dollars an hour or whatever the going rate is.

Design Objectives

Your first objective is to moisten the entire court area by turning on as few valves as possible, preferably only one. A second objective, if you live in a climate where pipes are subject to freezing, is to be able to drain the system easily.

Coverage

Covering the court area fully with the sprinklers depends on three things: water pressure, the number of sprinkler heads, and the positioning of the sprinkler heads.

Figure 41 indicates an ideal design for a system that is dependent on achieving an arc of water from each of five sprinkler heads of about 37½ feet. Through discussion with your plumber and/or your plumbing-supply house, try to find sprinkler heads that will throw water in that arc, given your water pressure, with all five heads operating simultaneously.

If your water pressure is too low to achieve this, then you will

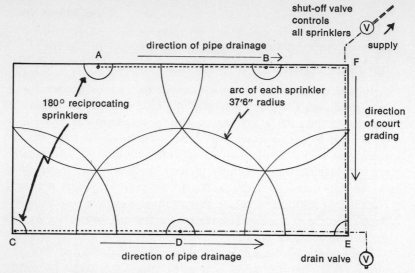

direction of pipe drainage

A

B →

F

180° reciprocating
sprinklers

arc of each sprinkler
37'6" radius

direction
of court
grading

C

D

E

direction of pipe drainage

drain valve ⓥ

FIGURE 41. One-valve system

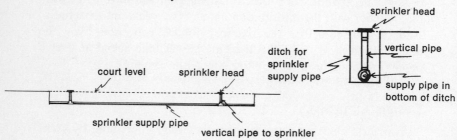

sprinkler head

ditch for
sprinkler
supply pipe

vertical pipe

supply pipe in
bottom of ditch

court level   sprinkler head

sprinkler supply pipe

vertical pipe to sprinkler

FIGURE 41A. Cutaway views showing details of sprinkler system

FIGURE 42. Two-valve system

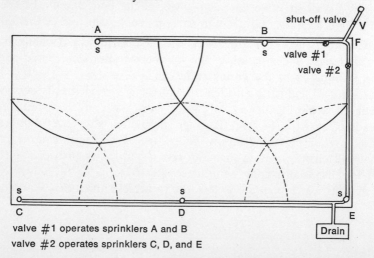

shut-off valve ⓥ

A

B

F

s

s

valve #1

valve #2

s

s

s

C

D

E

Drain

valve #1 operates sprinklers A and B
valve #2 operates sprinklers C, D, and E

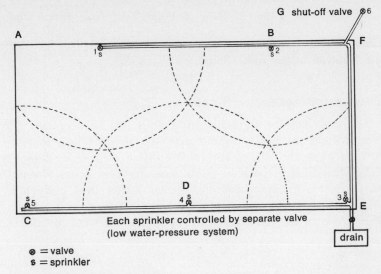

FIGURE 43. Six-valve system

not be able to operate all five at the same time, and you will have to compromise. If you can operate three at one time and attain the arc, then you can put the system on two valves (see Figure 42). If you can only operate one or two heads at a time, you will have to resort to a six-valve system (see Figure 43). It costs more to put in the additional joints and valves, but it is still worthwhile.

Draining the Pipes

In order to drain the pipes, you will need to put in a drain valve and to plan your system with a very slight grade. Dig a small pit for the drain valve, and put gravel at the bottom (see Figure 44). You can line the pit with cement blocks and put a precast

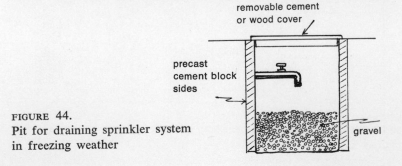

FIGURE 44.
Pit for draining sprinkler system
in freezing weather

cement cover or a wooden cover on it. A pit about two feet deep and eighteen inches wide should be adequate.

Ditches for Sprinkler Pipes

The ditch for the sprinkler pipes need not be very deep. In order to give the pipe sufficient drainage, grade 1 inch in every 20 feet. Thus, the pipe at sprinkler position A must be 3 inches higher than that at position B; B must be 1½ inches above D and F, which in turn must be 3 inches higher than position E. Therefore, A is 7½ inches higher than E. C is 6 inches higher than E. For a suggested guide to the levels you want to achieve,

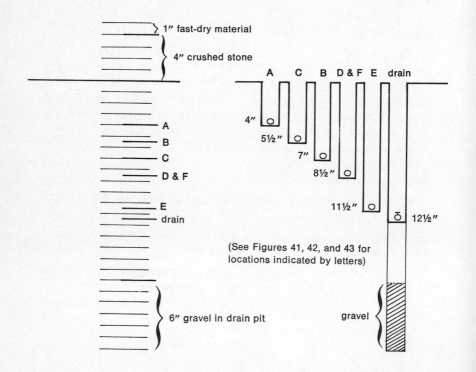

FIGURE 45. Relative depth of sprinkler pipe ditching at various locations in system

see Figure 45. This is based on the recommendation that the level of your fast-dry court be 5 inches above the surrounding terrain.

The ditch for the sprinkler pipe (see Figure 41) should be six inches inside the edge of the court to give you working space between the sprinkler heads and the brick curb you will be putting in next. After laying the pipe, with T-outlets for the five sprinkler heads, screw a short vertical piece of pipe into each outlet and cap it. Then place a stake off the court to mark the position of each of the heads (except the corner ones, which will be easily located). Then refill the ditches and tamp and roll the earth back to the original level and compaction. The sprinkler heads will not be installed until you have completed the fast-dry material, the brick curbing, and the fencing.

The Brick Curb

The porous court should be five to six inches above the surrounding ground level to promote better drainage and to prevent ground water from running into the court. The neatest way to retain the crushed-stone base and the fast-dry material is to install a brick curbing around the perimeter of the court. This of course must be done before you lay the crushed stone base.

Construct the curb by laying bricks flat, end to end, in a layer of cement, floating on enough gravel or crushed stone to bring the curb level up to the level of the stone base you will install next. In other words, the top of the brick should be four inches

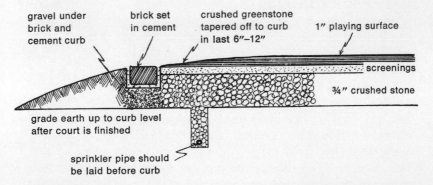

FIGURE 46. The brick curb and sprinkler pipe for the porous court

above the earth subbase (see Figure 46). Use the transit and a straightedge to be sure that the curb attains the desired height.

Use enough cement to hold the gravel and the brick but avoid carrying the cement down to the earth level. Doing so would slow the drainage of water from the stone base into the earth around the court. Leave a temporary opening in the curb for trucks and other heavy equipment and fill it in later.

The Rock Base (porous court)

Screed Strips

The rock base for the porous court consists of 4 inches of ¾-inch stone, filled and leveled with a 1-inch layer of screenings. However, to bring the stone base of the porous court to the desired level, you use a different method from the one described in Chapter 6 for the nonporous court. The method involves the installation of screed strips between which the crushed stone will be laid and leveled.

A screed strip is a strip of wood the same depth as the desired depth of the material you are laying. In this case, since you are laying 4 inches of stone, you will need enough 4-inch-by-1-inch pine boards to make seven complete rows the length of the court —that is, 840 running feet—*unless* you have installed brick curbing, in which case your curbing will serve the purpose of the outside screed strips and you will need only 600 running feet of the pine boards. However, this will only work if your curb height is extremely accurate (4 inches above the subbase). If you have any doubt about this, drive your stakes (as discussed below) and run your screed strips just inside the curbing, ignoring the curbing for the purpose of leveling.

Drive lengthwise rows of stakes (1 by 2 by 12 inches, pine) into the ground until the top of each stake is at exactly the height you will want for the compacted rock base. Check the height of each stake with rod and transit. Drive in a stake every 6 or 7 feet along the length of the court, to give the screed strips good support. Then nail the strips into the sides of the stakes, so the tops of the strips are flush with the tops of the stakes (see Figure 47). The screed strips should be 10 feet apart, measuring from center to center. To obtain a standard grade of 1 inch in 20 feet from side

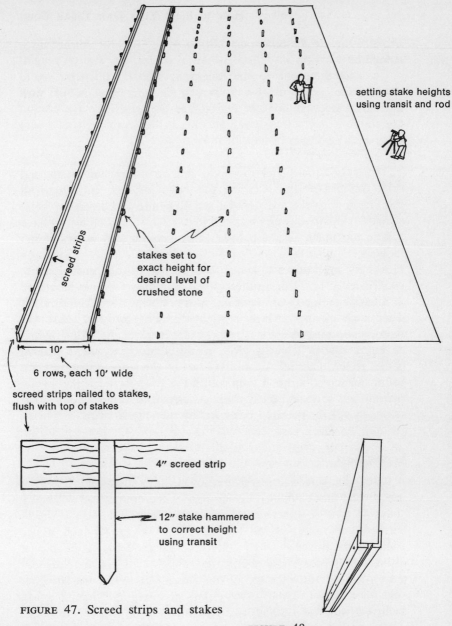

setting stake heights
using transit and rod

screed strips

stakes set to
exact height for
desired level of
crushed stone

10'

6 rows, each 10' wide

screed strips nailed to stakes,
flush with top of stakes

4" screed strip

12" stake hammered
to correct height
using transit

FIGURE 47. Screed strips and stakes

FIGURE 48
Straightedge, 2" × 12" × 12'
with angle irons nailed or
screwed to one edge

to side, the height difference between the rows of screed strips should be ½ inch.

To level the stone to the height of the screed strips, use a straightedge: a 2-inch-by-12-inch-by-12-foot pine board with angle iron screwed along one edge (see Figure 48).

The ¾-inch Stone

The truck should back down the first row, raise the dump, and drive forward slowly, releasing the stone just fast enough to fill the first row to the level of the strips. Guide the driver by hand signals to dump slower or faster if necessary. It's better to have a little too much than too little, since leveling off is easier than filling in.

Ask the truckdriver to leave an extra pile of the crushed stone; you'll need it to fill the spaces after you remove the screed strips.

Set your crew to work leveling the stone with shovels and rakes. Then, with a helper, pull the straightedge along two rows of screed strips, smoothing the stone to the exact level of the strips. When an entire row of stone is level, compact the row with a 1,000-pound roller. This will lower the level of the stone about ½ inch below the screed strips. Complete all the rows between the screed strips in this way until the court is covered with compacted ¾-inch stone, except for the area occupied by the screed strips.

Screenings

Before the screed strips are removed, have a supply of screenings (stone dust) dumped at one end of the court. You will need about 46 tons of screenings to cover the court area. Using wheelbarrows and rakes, spread the screenings on the ¾-inch stone. Some of the material will fill in the crevices between the pieces of ¾-inch stone. There should be enough to bring the level of the screenings up to the top of the screed strips. Use the straightedge once more to level the screenings precisely and then compact each row with the 1,000-pound roller.

Remove all the stakes and strips and fill the empty spaces first with the extra crushed rock and then with screenings, being careful to disturb the surface as little as possible. Tamp the rows as you fill them.

When you have finished filling and tamping, roll the entire court once more.

Fast-Dry Surface Material

Ordering the Material

Fast-dry surface material is made by a very few manufacturers because the stone itself is available only in certain areas of the East and must be shipped around the country. The companies are listed in Appendix A. The material is a crushed crystalline green-stone, specially treated to make it bind well.

The manufacturers recommend that you use about forty tons of the material to achieve a layer of 1¼ inches, which compacts to 1 inch with a 600-pound roller. The companies will ship it by the carload, which is impractical for the amateur builder, or in eighty-pound bags. One thousand of these bags will give you just forty tons.

When the material arrives, you must store the bags someplace where they will not get wet. If you don't have a shed or garage, a platform of boards and a covering of tarpaulins should suffice if you are careful.

Handling the Fast-Dry Material

You will need several helpers for this operation: some to move the bags of material onto the court by wheelbarrow, others to spread and level the material as it arrives.

Caution your workers to walk carefully on the stone dust as they work.

New Set of Screed Strips

The screed strips used to level the fast-dry material are completely different from those used for the ¾-inch stone and the screenings.

These screed strips are 3 to 4 inches in width, 1¼ inches thick, 20 feet long (less if 20-foot board is unavailable), and made of redwood so they will resist warping when damp. They are laid flat, rather than on edge. You should have sufficient lumber to

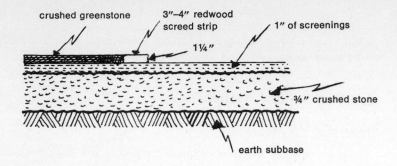

FIGURE 49. Cross section of the porous court with screed strip in place for applying crushed greenstone

border one complete row of material, or, in other words, at least 240 feet (see Figure 49).

Line up the strips along one side of the court and then place another line parallel to the first, measuring ten feet from center to center of the strips.

Applying the Material

Using wheelbarrows with pneumatic (air-filled) rubber tires if possible, wheel the bags of fast-dry material to the end of the first row and empty the bags between the strips.

Rake the material roughly level and slightly higher than the screed strips. After filling and roughly-leveling each ten to twelve feet of the row, draw the straightedge along the screed strips to level the material to the strips.

Continue in this fashion to fill the row from one end to the other.

Watering

As you move down the row, put one person to work watering it. Your helper should start where you began to lay the material and soak it thoroughly, using a hose with a spray nozzle, so that the water displaces the material as little as possible.

Experiment at the beginning to see how much watering it takes to penetrate the full depth of the fast-dry material. *You must dampen it thoroughly before rolling.*

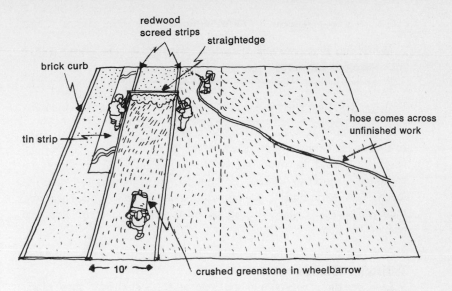

FIGURE 50. Leveling crushed greenstone with straightedge and screed strips

It is important to water from the unfinished side of the court, so that the hose does not disturb the fast-dry material. Note that in Figure 50 the hose comes across the unfinished court. Plan for this before you decide where to start laying the material.

Rolling the Fast-Dry Material

Before the dampened fast-dry material has had a chance to dry, it should be rolled with a 500- or 600-pound roller. This means you'll need another skilled member of your team to follow the hose person with the rolling.

It is essential that the rolling closely follow the watering. If you do not have enough workers to lay the material, water it, and roll it all at once, use your workers to finish laying down one complete row, *then* put them to work watering and rolling immediately.

Keep track of your time and pace the work so you can finish wetting and compacting all the material that you lay on any one day. Once it has been wet and rolled it will hold its position quite well. When it is loose, it is more vulnerable to wind and rain.

When the first row has been laid, leveled, watered, and rolled, move the outside screed strips to form another row.

Filling In for the Screed Strips

Each time you lift a line of screed strips and move the strips to their next position, you must fill the gap they leave. To do this, carefully trowel in material, smooth it slightly higher than the compacted material around it, water it thoroughly, and tamp it level. You may find that you will have to add a bit here and there or scrape a bit away in order to level the strip with the rest of the row.

Sprinkler Heads

As you finish compacting the fast-dry material at each edge of the court, locate the position for the sprinkler heads, dig down to the pipe, displacing as little material as possible, and install the sprinkler heads. Then replace the material around the sprinkler heads and tamp it smooth.

The Tin Strip

A tin strip twelve inches wide by ten to twelve feet long will prevent your straightedge from scraping the already compacted row next to where you are working, and it will also catch any excess material that the straightedge pushes ahead of it. Lay it in the position indicated in Figure 50.

As you finish using the straightedge on each portion of a row, move the tin strip along to the next portion.

Final Rolling

When you have finished laying, leveling, watering, and rolling the fast-dry material over the entire court area, including the gaps left by the removal of the strips, water the entire court and roll it again with the six-hundred-pound roller. If you find any spots that seem off level, either fill them or scrape them down carefully and roll the area again.

8.

Net Posts

I tend to be almost fanatic about the need for an enormous anchor for the net posts. And that's because I've known too many unhappy court owners with net-post problems like the one in Figure 51 to let you risk the same fate. As you know from the net-post plugs, the anchor should be thirty inches in diameter. The other vital dimension is the depth, which should be a full thirty-six inches.

There are those who have the temerity to suggest that a plug eighteen inches in diameter and twenty-four inches deep will hold a net post under proper tension without pulling out of the ground. With luck, it would last through the first summer. Even where there is no frost, it would gradually work its way up and over with the constant, unremitting pull of the net cable.

The USTA and the United States Tennis Court and Track Builders Association recommend that anchors be a *minimum* of twenty-four inches in diameter at the top, thirty inches in diameter at the bottom, and thirty-six inches deep. As long as you've gone that far, I suggest going to the thirty-inch width at the top, too. It adds weight and bulk at the fulcrum point (see Figure 52)

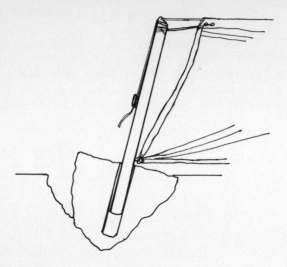

FIGURE 51. Inadequate net-post anchor

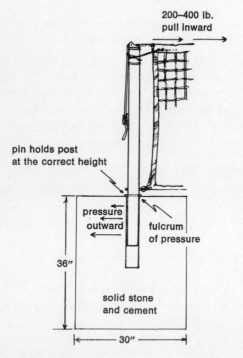

FIGURE 52. Net-post anchor

and will help to defeat any tendency of the post to be pulled inward at ground level.

Meeting my requirements doesn't add a great deal of time or material to the original installation. But it is very difficult to correct the problem five years after the court has been finished.

Time

8 person-hours per hole

Work Force

You
1 or 2 helpers (I would advise against doing it alone. Positioning the posts and setting them vertical is difficult to accomplish alone.)

Tools and Materials

Ball of good, heavy cotton mason's cord (porous court only)
Chalked snap line (nonporous court only)
6-foot folding wooden rule
Hammer
Nails (finishing)
Keel (lumberman's yellow marking crayon)
Carpenter's level
Tin snips
10-by-12-foot tarpaulins (2)
Mason's wheelbarrow (for moving dirt, mixing cement)
Pick (or 2 if you have the workers)
Long-handled shovels (2)
Short-handled shovels (2)
Post-hole digger (or 2)
Hoe (for mixing cement)
Net posts
Net-post sleeves (one supplied with each post you buy)
Aluminum flashing, 5 by 5 inches (2 pieces)
½-inch pipe, 20 inches long
Cement (approximately 14 bags for each hole)
Washed sand for mixing with cement (approximately 2½ yards for each hole)

Source of clean water (hose or bucket)

Fieldstones (if not available, 1½-inch crushed rock will do well)

Pine (or other wood) 4 feet long or more (2 straight pieces to position post exactly)

Masking tape (to hold cap on post sleeve)

Weather

DIGGING

Any

CEMENT WORK

50 degrees or above (light rain okay but when you reach finished top level, cover cement with plastic tarpaulin or other protection, to prevent washing away while curing)

Work Procedure

Spread a tarpaulin next to the net-post hole, toward one end of the court, so that it doesn't interfere with measurements from one side of the court to the other (see Figure 53). Then remove the net-post plugs by breaking them up with picks as much as necessary to get them out.

Dig the hole a full thirty-six inches deep, piling the dirt on the tarpaulin or if you have help, having it wheeled away in the wheelbarrow. But save whatever stones you find, for later use in the cement. Hose them off so they will be relatively free of dirt. If you run into a rock ledge much before the hole is complete, you should cement the net-post anchor to the rock. Hose off the rock surface enough so that the cement will come into contact with rock and not just dirt.

Assuming that you've reached the thirty-six-inch depth without any problem, scoop out a hollow at the center of the hole and put a little pile of gravel into it. This is where the pipe will drain from the sleeve. To prepare the sleeve for placement, cut out a piece of flashing or tin, as illustrated in Figure 54 (inset). Bend the flaps up around the sleeve to form a cap and then tape the cap over the bottom of the sleeve. This will prevent the sleeve from filling with wet cement. Cut a hole in the center of the cap

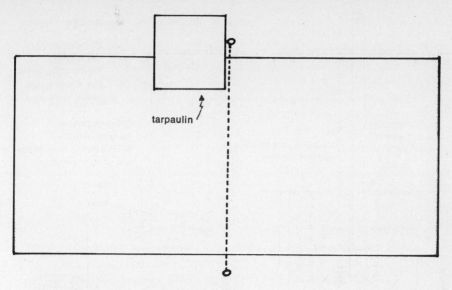

FIGURE 53. Placement of the tarpaulin

so that the ½-inch drainpipe can extend up at least an inch into the sleeve.

Be sure you have a good pile of fieldstone or crushed rock to work with. You'll want to have it handy for use as soon as you've mixed the cement.

Mix a batch (two parts sand to one part cement) in the wheelbarrow (which should be clean) or in a mortar box if you have one. The cement should be on the wet side, so that it will settle into all the crevices of the rocks you will put into it. Put a thick layer (two or three inches) of wet cement into the bottom of the holes. Avoid putting cement over the gravel in the center until the next layer when we will have put the drainpipe in place. Otherwise cement would block the drain. Then place stones in the cement, leaving space between the stones so you will be able to push cement down between them. The end result should be cement and stones with no air pockets. In placing the rocks, again leave room for the drainpipe at the center (see Figure 55). Stand the pipe in the gravel and with small stones and cement, build up around the pipe enough so that it will stand up fairly well. You will have to adjust it as you work.

You will continue to add rocks and cement, layer by layer, so

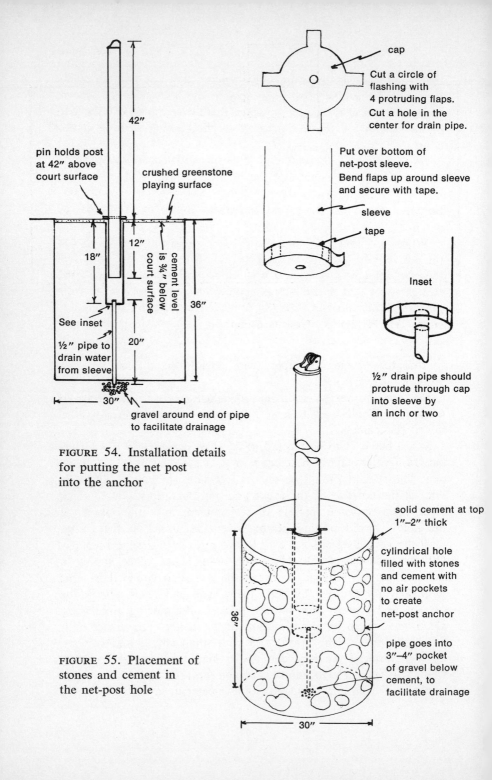

cap

Cut a circle of flashing with 4 protruding flaps. Cut a hole in the center for drain pipe.

Put over bottom of net-post sleeve. Bend flaps up around sleeve and secure with tape.

sleeve

tape

Inset

½″ drain pipe should protrude through cap into sleeve by an inch or two

pin holds post at 42″ above court surface

crushed greenstone playing surface

42″

18″

12″

cement level is ¾″ below court surface

36″

See inset

½″ pipe to drain water from sleeve

20″

30″

gravel around end of pipe to facilitate drainage

FIGURE 54. Installation details for putting the net post into the anchor

solid cement at top 1″–2″ thick

cylindrical hole filled with stones and cement with no air pockets to create net-post anchor

36″

pipe goes into 3″–4″ pocket of gravel below cement, to facilitate drainage

30″

FIGURE 55. Placement of stones and cement in the net-post hole

that each rock is touching only cement and not another rock. Remember, the pipe must poke up into the bottom of the sleeve; so keep in mind the depth at which the sleeve must be imbedded in the cement—eighteen inches from the playing surface of the court.

As you build in cement and stone around the sleeve, position it so that the pipe penetrates the hole in the cap. You may have to use a hammer to tap the pipe where you want it as you position the sleeve vertically and center it exactly in line with the net line.

When you have stone and cement four or five inches up around the sleeve, you must make an accurate check on its position. Put the post into the sleeve, and with someone holding the post, use straightedges and a level to get the sleeve into exactly the right position. Then lift the post out and continue adding cement and stone (see Figure 56). Before being fully committed to the sleeve position, insert the post once more and make another check of alignment.

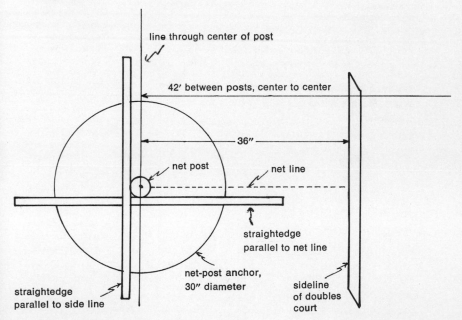

FIGURE 56. Positioning the net post

When you are within a few inches of filling the hole, you may need smaller stones. The final two inches or so should be solid cement. Remember to keep the level of the cement ¼ inch below the asphalt level or with a porous court 1 inch below the playing surface.

When the hole is filled, with the cement up to the prescribed level, make a final check of the sleeve by again putting the post in place.

A reminder: The most important aspect of this operation is the accurate positioning of the sleeve and post. The drainpipe is a great convenience, but if for some reason you have to sacrifice it in order to properly position the sleeve and post, then sacrifice! You can always sponge out the water that gets into the net-post hole—I've been doing it with mine because I never thought of the drainpipe—but there is no way you can change the position of the sleeve once the cement hardens.

9.

Fencing

The nice thing about fencing is that it's an area where you can choose an inexpensive alternative without adversely affecting the qualities of play or the durability of the court. After five or ten years you can change to a more permanent fence without any disruption of the court surface.

Depending on the area surrounding the court, an inexpensive fence made of creosoted wood and chicken wire can blend into the background very well.

The Kinds of Fences

Wood and Chicken Wire

The least expensive fence materials are creosoted pine and chicken wire. They will stand up for seven or eight years and do a good job if installed properly.

Hardware Cloth

Hardware cloth is much more durable than chicken wire and sturdier under accidental impact—for example, with a player in hot pursuit of a deep lob. A top grade, galvanized, will be good for fifteen or twenty years. The cost will be roughly double that of chicken wire.

Cyclone Fencing

Cyclone fencing is by far the sturdiest, most durable, and most expensive. It is also difficult to put up. In fact, I recommend having it done by professionals, after comparing estimates from several companies in your area. It is possible to purchase the materials and do it yourself but it requires special tools and is extremely hard work.

The Design of Your Fence

The design of the fencing—that is, whether it will run all around the court, be lower on the sides, be open at the sides, or combine any of these choices—will depend on the terrain surrounding the court, the money you want to spend, and the esthetic choices you will want to make.

Height of the Fence

Unless a zoning or building code or some other irreversible problem prevents it, your fencing should be twelve feet high at the ends and continue at that height for at least twenty feet along each side. A regulation tennis ball, when lobbed high to the baseline or slammed down on the court by an overhead, will often sail over a ten-foot fence. But very few legal bounces will clear the twelve-footer.

The USTA also makes this height recommendation, but if you try to buy twelve-foot cyclone fencing, you may meet with opposition by the fence company, which may not keep it in stock. Stick to your guns. You *need* the height, and you know better than they. When the salesman says, *"Everyone* uses ten-foot fence," you tell him that's because everyone gets talked into it by fence companies.

At the sides of the court, there are a number of options open to you, depending on the character of the area surrounding the court (see Figure 57). If you have deep brush that will make it difficult to find a lost ball, then you ought to continue your fencing,

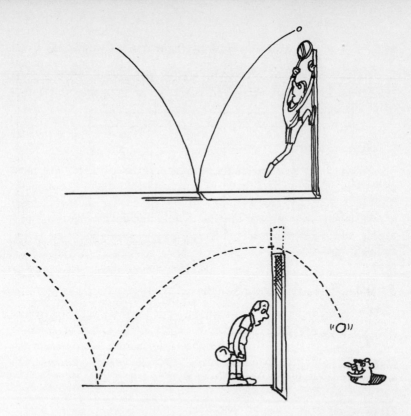

You can usually retrieve the balls that go over a ten-foot fence. Your temper is harder to recover.

using an eight-to-ten-foot height along that side. If, on the other hand, there is open lawn next to the court, you can eliminate fencing on that side or if you prefer, use a four-foot height.

We wanted to have our court feel as open as possible, while still maintaining control over the balls. On one side our lawn slopes upward, away from the court, and no ball rolls very far uphill. We even broke a cardinal rule by reducing the length of the side fence to twelve feet at each end. However, we did slant our fencing outward slightly, to catch more of the wide-hit serves or drives. On the brook side of our court, we installed green nylon netting eight feet high; it is virtually invisible but stops *almost* all balls from going into the brook. The flowers, rocks, and trees stop many balls. The openness of the court, surrounded by greenery

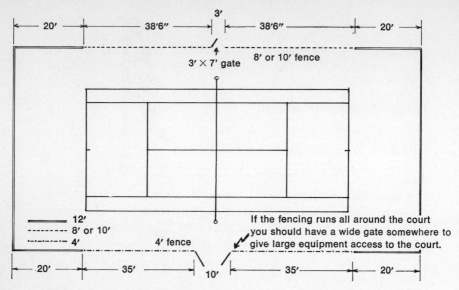

FIGURE 57. Fencing of different heights, depending on what surrounds or adjoins the court

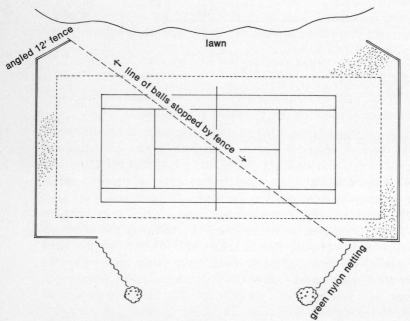

FIGURE 58. The Anderson Court

and lawn, is so pleasing, it has a calming effect even on those whose games are "off" (see Figure 58).

Installation Information

Chicken Wire or Hardware Cloth

Posts
4-by-4-inch posts, no knots, redwood or cypress; corner posts 30 inches into ground in cement plugs at least 18 inches wide; other posts 24 inches into ground in cement plugs at least 12 inches wide; posts should be spaced every 10 feet.

Rails and Bracing
2-by-4-inch lumber, no knots, redwood, cypress, or pine; place just above ground for better weathering.

Wire
Good galvanized wire or vinyl-coated if you want to spend a little more for greater durability; staple wire to posts and rails; wire tight to ground below rail.

Weatherproofing
All wood should be protected against weather with paint, stain, or creosote appropriate for the wood you choose.

(See Figures 59 and 60 for details.)

Cyclone Fencing

Posts
3-inch corner posts, other posts 2½ inches; corner posts 30 inches into ground in cement plugs at least 18 inches wide; other posts 24 inches into ground in cement plugs at least 12 inches wide; good grade of galvanized pipe for all posts.

Rails and Bracing
1¾-inch galvanized pipe.

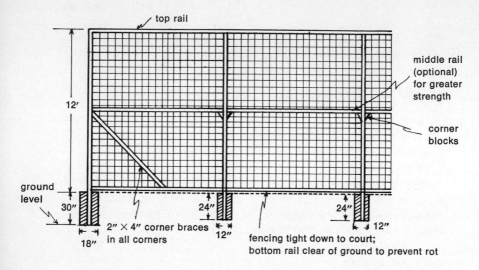

FIGURE 59. Portion of fence of hardware cloth or chicken wire and 4″ × 4″ posts

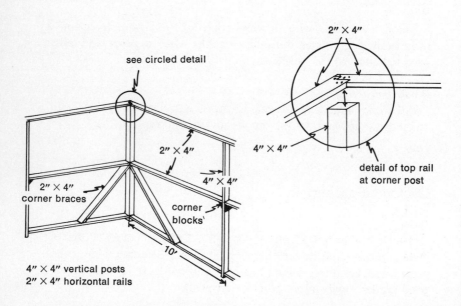

FIGURE 60. Wooden frame for hardware cloth or chicken wire fence (details)

Wire
Cyclone fencing, either galvanized or vinyl-clad in color of your choice.

Weatherproofing
None needed.

Installation Difficulties
Putting in posts is arduous but can be done with time and muscle; putting wire on it requires stretchers to pull wire tight from pole to pole; heavy rolls take a lot of manpower to hold roll upright as you unroll it from post to post, fastening it to each post in turn.

Recommendations
Consider pricing job at various fencing contractors in your neighborhood; if you install posts yourself, you can cut a great deal of labor cost.

"WE COULD HAVE . . ."

"The M.G.s want us for a quick lunch tomorrow—they know we're working—and the Rossins want us for dinner at 6:30."

"Fine," I said. "We'll rake in the morning, seed and roll in the afternoon, take a nap, and be ready for dinner."

And thus, for the first time, I defied Robert Pirsig's rule about not giving yourself deadlines when you're doing a job you've never done before.

After Sunday breakfast I checked the grass seed, which I had spread on the garage floor to dry after soaking it for the recommended four hours, and we started our fine-grading with rakes.

We raked and raked, and as the time flew by, I realized that I did not dare stop for lunch. Nancy phoned our regrets, we had yogurt, and we kept going. By the middle of the afternoon, I was beginning to panic. I pushed myself as hard as I could, ignored my sore hands, and raked blindly on. We had to finish because the soaking had started the germination of the seed.

In the late afternoon I asked Nancy to cancel our dinner date and stumbled onward, with the loathsome rake in my aching hands.

As the sun set, at about 7:30, we began to cast the grass seed. After casting an area, we had to rake it lightly. Then I pulled the roller over it and Nancy sprayed it carefully with the garden hose. On and on, into darkness, we spread, raked, rolled, and watered—until finally, it was dark and we could no longer see the seed falling. We turned the headlights of both cars on the area and continued numbly. Sometime before 11:00, we had finished—blistered, exhausted, long past hunger, not sure how well we had done the last two hours of work by headlight.

Looking back on it, I know we could have enlisted help ahead of time. We could have had the raking completed before soaking the seed. We could have—we could have listened to Pirsig.

10.

Landscaping

You have almost certainly had to disturb the landscape when you put in your court. You may have left great scars of raw earth, exposed rock, or steep banks of earth to wash away. However you have scarred the landscape, you must repair the damage before you can consider the job finished. You will enjoy your court far more if it adds to the attractiveness of your place.

Retaining Walls

On pages 77–78 we dealt with the need for retaining walls when you have a sharp drop near the court edge and so must prevent the eventual washing and settling that could take place otherwise. You should also put in walls if you have made steep cuts in the earth that may wash *toward* the court.

Trees

You may have had to cut down trees that were an attractive part of your home. If you now feel you should plant some young trees in the area surrounding the court, make sure to look ahead. A tree reaching a particular height may create shadow problems if it is on the east, south, or west of the court perimeter.

Also be sure that fully developed root systems will not grow into the court area. Remember that the roots of a tree reach out at least as far from the trunk as do the branches. A growing root will lift and crack the best-laid asphalt.

However, trees may offer valuable wind protection for the court. Study the area when the wind is blowing to judge how much of a problem wind may be. Save any trees that provide wind protection, as long as their root systems will not reach the court area. You may want to plant some fast-growing evergreens or deciduous trees for windbreak. Evergreens have the advantage of protecting the court throughout the year.

Shrubs, Hedges, and Bushes

You may want to put in shrubs, or bushes. They can serve several purposes: to stop balls that may roll away from the court if you do not have fencing all around it; to shield the court from wind; to cut off a view of and from the court that might prove disturbing for a neighbor or for a player; and finally, for their attractiveness.

Grass

Grass is the most practical and pleasing way to join the court to the area around it. This will be especially true if you are one of those who has chosen an asphalt court with the grass-strip alternative (see pages 94–96).

As soon as you have graded the raw earth around the court area to your satisfaction, you should get grass growing as quickly as possible, to keep the earth from washing away.

Time

Flexible (each case different, but allow ample time; raking, seeding, and rolling are done best when you're not trying to meet a deadline)

Work Force

You

0–20 helpers, depending on the size of the area you have to put in shape and the number of rakes available; for a plot of any size, you should have at least 4 or 5.

Tools, Equipment, and Materials

Bulldozer (if you must move large amounts of rock or earth)
Truck (if you have to bring earth in or take it away from the court site)
Metal hand rakes, as final tool for shaping, smoothing, and putting in grass (1 per worker)
Hoes, as a valuable adjunct to rakes
Shovels (as needed)
Picks (as needed)
Mattocks (as needed)
Crowbar (as needed)
Sledge hammer (as needed)
Lawn roller, hand-pulled
8-inch tamper
Topsoil (if needed)
Grass seed (as needed)
Trees (as needed)
Bushes (as needed)

Outline of the Job

Rough-grading
Fine-grading
Seeding
Watering

Rough-Grading

Essentially, rough-grading involves filling in earth where it is needed and hauling it away when there is an excess.

This part of the job calls on your aesthetic sense—your sense of balance, of design, of spatial relationships. Not everyone exercises these senses. You will have to decide whom to trust—yourself, your spouse, some other family member, or a friend whose taste you respect. The grading, curves, lines, levels, and shapes should be pleasing and should help to make the court look as though it *belongs* where it is and is not an intrusion on the landscape.

Rough-grading also requires that you anticipate what sort of drainage you will have when the land is shaped. Design the grading to carry running water from rainfall or melting snow around or away from the court as much as possible. You may want to employ the transit and rod to check on the levels involved, to be sure that you are not expecting water to run uphill.

Fine-Grading

When the bulldozer has done what rough-grading it can do, the handwork begins. In this case many hands *do* make light work. Tell all your friends to bring rakes, hoes, and shovels and then tell the inexperienced how to use the tools.

Use the tines of the rake to loosen the earth and the back of the rake to move it around and smooth it (see Figure 61). Use hoes to augment the rake when you want to cut and move more earth.

Be sure to tamp, stamp, or roll the filled-in areas as you work. If you leave an area for later, you may forget it until you are doing your final rolling. You may then discover you have a hollow that must be filled. So keep compacting as you work. You must achieve an even degree of compaction or soft spots will later sink.

The tines of the rake will continually discover rocks. Keep piling them up and hauling them away. They have many useful purposes—filling large holes, building drainage ditches, patching driveway potholes—but they don't belong in lawns. Even if you bury them in an inch of dirt, they will pop up a few months later and the lawnmower blades will hit them.

Keep softening, moving, and smoothing, then rolling or tamping. If need be, repeat the operation. Gradually the earth will assume the shape you want.

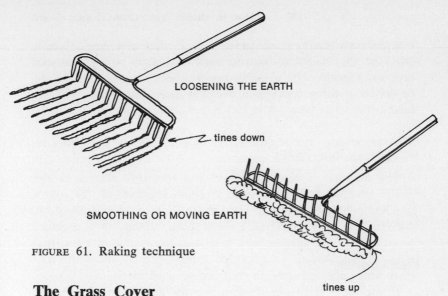

LOOSENING THE EARTH

— tines down

SMOOTHING OR MOVING EARTH

FIGURE 61. Raking technique

tines up

The Grass Cover

Choosing a Grass Seed

You will have to rely on your own knowledge or the knowledge of your local garden supply shops in picking out a grass seed. What you want is a grass that will take punishment and that will grow well in sunny areas. You also want a grass that has as long a growing season as possible.

Look for the best hardy grass seed you can buy. It is worth the extra initial expense to ensure a growth that will hold, cover, and adorn the earth for years and years to come. The only person who will profit from a bargain in grass seed is someone who is never going to have to live with the grass when it comes up—if it comes up. A developer, for instance.

Preparing the Seed

You can give grass seed a head start before putting it into the earth. Soak the seed in warm water (about 100 degrees Fahrenheit or 38 degrees Celsius (Centigrade), for about four hours. Then spread the seed out on a flat surface, like the cement floor of a garage, and leave it overnight. Sow it the next day—without fail—since having soaked the seed, you have begun the germination process. However, the advantage is that you don't have to wait for the chemicals in the earth to begin the germination process. Therefore, the grass will root more quickly and there will be less time for a heavy rain to wash away the loose earth and seed.

Preparing the Earth

The top two or three inches of soil (topsoil) should be rich in the minerals and elements that promote growth. If the topsoil is poor, you should spread fertilizer before or after seeding—or you can mix the fertilizer with the seed and spread them together. In either case, be sparing with fertilizer. Too much is worse than none. Again, consult your garden supply person about the kind of fertilizer and the strength that can be used safely.

If you don't have one, rent or borrow a spreader for the fertilizer or the fertilizer-seed combination. If you are seeding separately, you can do very well without the spreader by simply *casting*. In any case, casting is the best method on uneven ground or in confined areas.

Casting

Take a handful of seed and repeatedly swing your forearm and wrist in an arc, parallel to the ground, releasing a little seed each time your hand describes the arc. You will cast somewhat unevenly at first, until you have had practice. But no harm will be done by putting too much seed in an area; it's just wasteful. After working your way gradually over the area, check your work and add to spots where you find that you have scattered too little seed. Each square inch should average a minimum of 3 or 4 seeds and a maximum of 15 seeds. Remember, these are averages. Some unevenness will do no harm.

Raking and Rolling the Seed

As soon as the seed has been spread, it must be raked in. Draw the rake lightly over the earth, so that the tines penetrate about an inch. Support the weight of the rake with your forward hand to avoid digging any deeper. Each tine becomes a plow making a tiny furrow. Many of the seeds fall into the furrows.

When the raking is done, push the lawn roller over the entire area. As the roller flattens the softened earth, many of the seeds will be buried in a thin layer of earth. Some will still be on the surface and may never germinate. But experience shows that enough of the seed is buried to do the job. If there are areas where it is difficult to use the roller, the tamper will achieve the same result.

Watering

As soon as you have rolled the seed in, you should water the seeded area thoroughly. You must apply enough water so that it soaks down below the seed—to a depth of at least two inches. But you must do this gradually, using only a fine spray; otherwise, the water will wash away the earth and expose the seed that you have so carefully covered.

Repeat the watering each day for the next two days, then every three or four days, until the grass is standing. The first shoots will begin to appear on the third or fourth day if you have soaked the seed before planting. It may otherwise take a few days more, depending on the temperature, the composition of the earth, and the vigor of the seed.

The grass may look thin in spots and heavy in others, especially if you've had rain that did a little washing. Don't panic. Most of your area will fill in rapidly. And if there are bald spots because of seed washed by rain, it is easy to rake, seed, and roll those spots. They will catch up quickly.

Cutting

Before very long you will have to mow the grass or it will begin to fall over and matt. Young grass is thin and tender, and the shoots will not hold themselves erect when they are much over 2½ inches. At the same time, the earth is still soft; so you should use a light mower, doing as little damage to the earth as possible. After mowing, you can roll the new lawn once more, using a very light roller if the earth seems soft. The shoots will stand up after a day or so.

When To Plant

In most parts of the country it is best to plant grass, bushes, and trees either in the fall, after the growing period but a few weeks before first frost, or in the spring, when the frost is gone and the earth is waking up.

Since it is likely that you will finish work on your court sometime during the summer or early fall, you should get the grass started as soon as possible, so that it will hold the earth through the winter. Trees and bushes can wait until the following spring or fall if that is more convenient.

The Hidden Values of Landscaping

We've had players say, "You know, I just love to play on your court. It's so beautiful that even when I'm playing badly, I enjoy myself." To be sure, there have been some complaints, too. For instance, "Those damn ducks made me take my eye off the ball!" And we have one good friend who swears that we put the rose bushes on the fence to inhibit him when he goes back for a lob. It's true he did bleed quite a lot when we pulled him loose.

11.

Net and Lines

It's time to establish the great obstacles of the game: the net and the lines. After all, the whole game involves hitting a ball over the former and within the latter.

The Net

Buy a net of very good quality. The least expensive nets tend to skimp not only on the weight and durability of the material but on the size. Therefore, they do not fulfill the Rules of Tennis, as described by the USTA. Inexpensive nets not only deteriorate quickly. The manufacturers often save on material, resulting in a net which does not cover the prescribed area adequately. So it's really not a saving to buy anything but a very good net. A heavy-duty nylon net, with a nylon band along the top and supported by a steel cable, should last for many years without any special care.

The net should fit snugly from post to post and to the court when it is in proper position. The posts for the doubles court are forty-two inches high and forty-two feet apart, from *center to center*. Since you will want to play both singles and doubles, it is simplest to use a doubles net at all times (see Figure 62).

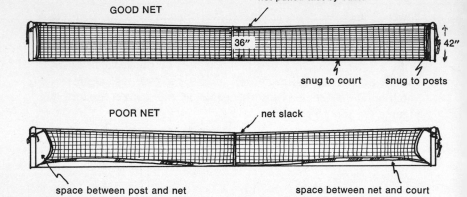

FIGURE 62. A poor net does not meet USTA standards.

There is no need to loosen a nylon net between uses or to take it down in the winter if you are planning to use the court during the cold months. Nylon is not harmed by being under constant tension. However, if your net is made of cotton, slack it off when it is not in use. Shrinking and stretching will wear it out if it is kept taut all the time. Also, a cotton net must be tested for height each time you play.

Net Stick

To check the height of the net at the center strap, cut a stick or old broom handle to exactly forty-two inches in length and put a notch in it at exactly thirty-six inches. With the net fairly taut and the net strap in place, one person should hold the stick next to the strap at net-center while another adjusts the strap so that it holds the net firmly at the height of the notch on the net stick (see Figure 63).

Singles Sticks

If you are a perfectionist, you may want to adhere precisely to USTA regulations for the height of the net in singles play. This means supporting the net to the forty-two-inch height at a point three feet outside the singles lines. To do this, cut two pieces of dowel, 1 inch in diameter, 42 inches long. Cut a ¼-inch notch in the top and wedge the notch under the net cable, so that the sticks are vertical and exactly three feet from the singles lines. With a ruler check the height of the top of the net cable above the sticks. If it is higher than 42 inches, increase the depth of the notch until the stick holds the cable at the correct height (see Figures 64 and 65).

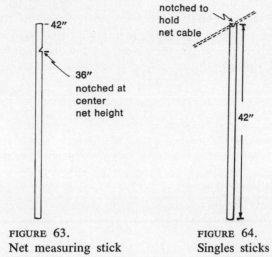

FIGURE 63.
Net measuring stick

FIGURE 64.
Singles sticks

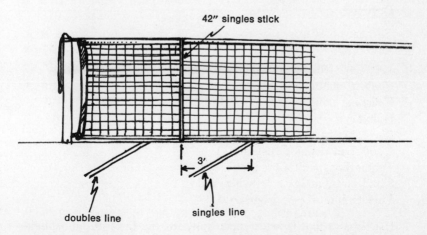

FIGURE 65. Placement of the singles sticks

The Lines

Lining the Nonporous Court

As I explained previously, lining the court at this point is optional. You will have to repeat the procedure after you apply the asphaltic-emulsion playing surface. However, I assume that if you love tennis enough to build your own court, you won't want to wait until the asphalt has cured before you start playing. If you do decide to wait, simply follow these instructions after applying the playing surface.

Time

1 day

Work Force

You
2 helpers (for layout)
1 helper (for painting lines)

Weather

Dry

Tools

100-foot steel measuring tapes (2)
Chalked snapline
Finishing nails, 4 penny (2 dozen)
Hammer
Keel (lumberman's yellow marking crayon)
Good 2-inch paintbrushes (2)
Tennis line paint (1 gallon)
Small cans, at least 3 inches wide (2)
Line template (see Figure 66)

Use a paint that is made specifically for the lines on an asphalt-base court. These very durable acrylic latex paints will not harm the surface whereas oil paint, even a good one, will.

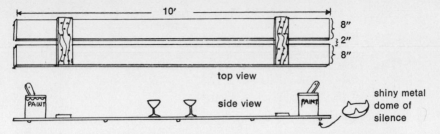

top view

side view

shiny metal
dome of
silence

With two pieces of 1″ × 4″ pine, nail two 1″ × 8″ × 10′ pieces of straight pine board parallel to each other, exactly 2″ apart. Use several nails or screws so that the two boards will be held rigidly. Fasten five domes of silence into the bottom of each 10′ board, to lift the boards slightly off court and prevent paint from smearing.

Treat the line template carefully, so that it will not be knocked out of true alignment.

In the side view I have illustrated the practical way to move the paint with you as you move the template to a new position. Do it with care, however. For an explanation of the two glasses, see page 145.

FIGURE 66. Line template

You established the position for the court lines when you positioned the net posts. If you did that job correctly (and I hope you did because any error is irremediable), it will be simple to mark out the position for the singles and doubles courts.

Layout for the Lines

Snap a line between the two net posts. From the center of each post measure and mark off 3 feet and 7½ feet. The first will be the outside of the doubles court, the second the outside of the singles court. Drive finishing nails at each point (see Figure 67).

Run one tape measure (tape 1) from point A toward C. Run the other tape measure (tape 2) diagonally from B toward C. Cross the tapes where tape 1 measures exactly 39 feet and tape 2 measures 47 feet, 5¼ inches. Make a mark at point C but do not drive a nail. You must check it.

To establish point D, run tape 1 from B toward D and tape 2 diagonally from A toward D. Cross them in the same manner as you did to find C. Make a mark at point D. Now run a tape from C to D. It should be exactly 27 feet. If it is off by as much as a quarter of an inch, recheck your diagonal measurements of 47 feet 5¼ inches and your side measurements of 39 feet to see why there is an error. When you are within ¼ inch, average out the error to make the line C–D exactly 27 feet and put nails in C and D.

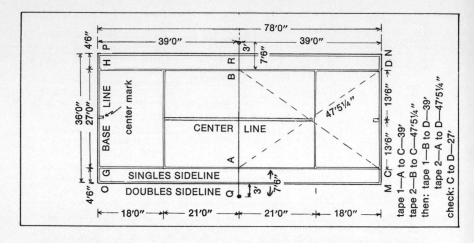

All measurements are made to the *outside* of the line, *except* the center line and the center marks, which are measured to their centers.
All lines are 2″ wide. Optional: the base lines may be as wide as 4″ if you want the extra visibility.

FIGURE 67. Layout for the lines

You can now run a measuring tape 39 feet from A toward G, snap a line that runs through C and A to G. Again, make a mark but do not drive a nail. Find point H in the same manner, then check the baseline G–H to be sure it is 27 feet. If it is not, check and remeasure to find the error and bring line G–H to a tolerance of ¼ inch before driving the marking nails.

Once the corners C, D, G, and H are established, it is an easy matter to establish the other points with the snapline and measuring tape. Mark carefully, and double-check all points before being satisfied.

Make clear snaplines to outline all the lines you will be painting. I suggest making them exactly two inches wide, although the USTA allows some exceptons to this rule. For instance, the baselines can be four inches wide if you prefer. They will then be easier to see from the opposite end of the court. Be sure the center lines and the center marks are exactly halfway between the two side lines. All other lines are measured to the *outside* edge of the line. The center marks should be six inches long from the *outside of the baseline*. This means they project four inches into the playing area beyond a two-inch baseline.

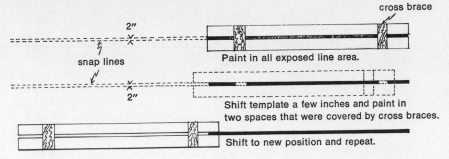

2″

snap lines

Paint in all exposed line area.

2″

Shift template a few inches and paint in
two spaces that were covered by cross braces.

Shift to new position and repeat.

FIGURE 68. Using the line template

Painting in the Lines

Because the *outside* edges of the baselines and the sidelines are
the most important boundaries, be sure to paint very clean, neat,
straight lines along your snapline. The inside edges of these same
lines are important but not quite as critical as the outside ones.
Start on an outside line of the doubles court at the net. By the
time you have reached the baseline you will have had enough
practice to be quite expert.

Lay the line template over the snapline (see Figure 68). You and
your helper should start at opposite ends of the template, painting
toward each other. Leave unpainted the portion that is blocked
by the cross-braces of the line template. When you have joined
your painting, lift the template and move it a few inches, to paint
in the portions that you left unpainted. Move the template along
the line to the next unpainted section and repeat. In this manner,
paint in all the lines.

If you wish to make the baselines wider than two inches, first
paint them in two inches wide and when they have dried, snap a
line to indicate the added thickness you desire. Then use the
template to add the additional width.

When the lines have dried, correct any important errors by
painting green, red, or black (depending on the color of your
surface) over any white paint that overflowed its line.

Inasmuch as the painting of the lines is the last official act you'll
perform before you can start to play, it seems only right that
there be some sort of small ceremony to commemorate it. To that
end, we made a pitcher of ice-cold martinis and carried it, with
two appropriate glasses, to the court. We found that the glasses
balanced on the line template quite as well as a small can of paint.
Finishing each ten-foot strip was rewarded by a sip of the silvery

concoction. I recommend, however, that this ceremony be postponed until you are painting the very last line.

Alternate Painting Method

An alternate method is to outline all the lines with ¾-inch masking tape, paint them in, and then remove the tape. This procedure is difficult on moderately rough asphalt but can be done quite successfully on the smoother asphaltic-emulsion playing surface, described in Chapter 12.

You will need 160 yards of tape, which is about three average rolls. If you get the tape down tight to the surface you can do a very neat job. But it may not be quite as interesting as using the template because there's no place to keep the martini glasses.

Lining the Porous Court

There are at least three kinds of tapes available for lining the porous, fast-dry court: leaded fabric, plastic, and metal. Leaded fabric or metal is best. The plastic may save you money, but it tends to tear more easily and does not have the weight to keep it lying flat.

You established the position for the lines when you positioned the net posts. If you did that job correctly (and I hope you did because any error is irremediable), it will be simple to mark out the position for the singles and doubles courts.

Time

1 day

Work Force

You
2 helpers (for the layout)
3 helpers (nailing down tapes)

Tools and Materials

100-foot steel measuring tapes (2)
Ball of good, heavy cotton cord (mason's cord)
3-inch aluminum nails (14 lbs.)
Hammers, carpenter's (3 or 4 depending on helpers)
Fabric or metal lining tape

Layout for the Lines

Follow the same procedure described on pages 143–144 for the nonporous court, with one exception: mark your points with a three-inch aluminum nail and do not drive it all the way in.

When you have established all the points, including those for the doubles court, begin by laying the tapes for the doubles sidelines and baselines (see Figure 68). Next, lay the sidelines for the singles court, then the service lines, and finally, the center line and center markers.

To find the position for each tape, pull the cord taut over two nail markers and fasten the cord to nails driven in *beyond* the marking point. To pull the cord taut, you will need to anchor it with several nails at the ends. Then carefully anchor the string every twenty or twenty-five feet, being careful not to push it out of line.

Using the cord as a guide, start the tape at one corner and nail down about three feet of tape to anchor it. Then pull the tape taut to the far point and holding it taut, put in several nails at the far end.

Being careful to keep tape aligned with the cord as you work, nail the tape down every two or three feet for its full length. Give the cord a little snap every once in a while to be sure it has not been pushed out of alignment.

Once the entire tape has been secured drive nails in all the nail holes, ordinarily three inches apart. Fully overlap the tape at all intersections. Nail through both layers of tape at the four outside corners of the doubles court, points M, N, O, and P.

When the tape is all down, roll the court thoroughly, making sure to go over all the tapes.

The Ceremony

Although there is no natural vehicle for the two glasses that climaxed the painting of the lines on the nonporous court, it would be unfair to deprive yourself of a celebration. So just bring the pitcher and glasses out for the final rolling. Or if you prefer, pull the cork on a bottle of champagne.

12.

The Nonporous Playing Surface

The final phase in surfacing the nonporous tennis court involves material with which most people are unfamiliar; in fact, this is one of the elements that makes tennis courts seem a mystery.

There are some rubbery synthetic and plastic surfacing materials that can be applied to an asphalt base but only with special equipment and by trained personnel. You would be required to contract for the application of any of these surfaces and the high cost would defeat your whole purpose, which is to build a good court at a great saving by doing most of the work yourself.

The surfacing material I recommend is an asphaltic emulsion that is applied cold, using thirty-inch rubber squeegees. Although there is some skill involved, you can easily master it. Asphaltic emulsion is a material made from a combination of asphalt, various fibers, and other substances that provide a relatively smooth, soft surface.

These emulsions are available in a choice of colors, although the least expensive one is black. Actually, since you will be applying a tennis-court paint in the color of your choice, the surface need not have a color. However, as the paint wears in spots, the emulsion may eventually show through; so you may find it's worth spending the few extra dollars.

You will have to follow the instructions that are provided by the individual manufacturer in respect to the proper dilution with water and the amount of material you should apply to each square foot of court.

General Rules for Application

Allow the asphalt base to cure for a minimum of four to six weeks and preferably sixty to ninety days before you apply the asphaltic-emulsion playing surface. The gases and solvents in the asphalt must be allowed to escape. As I warned above, if you trap them with the playing surface, they will bubble through gradually, partially—or even completely—destroying your beautiful surface.

Apply the asphaltic-emulsion playing surface only in warm, dry weather. The temperature should be above 50 degrees Fahrenheit (10 degrees Celsius) and climbing, not dropping. And there should be no threat of rain for a full twenty-four hours. The emulsion is a water-base material and will wash if exposed to rain before it is thoroughly dry. Fortunately, on a warm, sunny day it dries very rapidly. You will be able to tell by touching it.

The whole job should be done at one time. Therefore, you should have all the manpower and tools and materials ready before you begin.

Time

Flooding court (or waiting for rain to do it), draining and
   marking areas (3 hours)
Patching puddle areas (after court dries) (1 day)
Applying asphaltic-emulsion playing surface (1 day)
Applying color coat (4 hours)
Reapplying lines (see Chapter 11)

Work Force

You (to oversee all operations, make sure quantities are correct,
   land a hand when needed)
2 for squeegees

4 for mixing and pouring

1 for water hose (in case the court gets so hot that emulsion dries before it can be spread evenly)

1 for emergencies

Tools and Materials

30-inch rubber squeegees, long-handled, with deep blades (2, as illustrated in Figure 1)

Mixing poles, 2-by-3-inch, 4 feet long, sturdy (2)

Pliers and screwdriver (to open cans)

Garden hose with fine spray nozzle

Water pail

Straightedge (for patching)

Hand saw

Whisk broom

Keel (lumberman's yellow marking crayon)

5-cent piece, U.S.

Trowel

Asphaltic emulsion in 5-gallon cans for easy handling (quantity for court area as recommended by manufacturer)

Color coating in 5-gallon cans for easy handling (quantity per manufacturer's advice)

Patching material and fine sand or whatever advised by manufacturer (5 or 10 gallons will probably be enough)

Binder (if advised, to apply before patching an area)

Patching

Every effort was made in the asphalt layers to achieve a flat surface with no depressions deeper than $\frac{1}{16}$ inch in every ten feet. However, we may still find birdbaths if we flood the court or examine it after a rain.

When the court has stopped draining after a rain or after you've flooded it with a hose, take a keel and mark the perimeter of every depression that is holding water deeper than $\frac{1}{16}$ of an inch. Lay a nickel in the puddle. If the water covers the coin the depression is over the allowable depth and you'll need to patch.

Mix the patching material in accordance with the manufacturer's directions and start with the largest patch. Cut a piece of one-by-four-inch white pine board to the length of this patch; the board will serve as your straightedge.

Trowel the patching material into the low area and then work the straightedge over it until the area is leveled out to the yellow crayon boundary. Next cut the straightedge off to the length of the second-widest patch and proceed as before.

Before each patch dries, take a broom or whisk broom and drag it lightly over the area to give it a little roughness. Try to match the surface texture of the surrounding asphalt to some extent. You will probably not be able to get quite the same irregularity because you are not working with a crushed rock aggregate.

Applying Asphaltic Emulsion

Mixing

When the patching material is thoroughly dry, you are ready to apply the asphaltic-emulsion playing surface. All you need is warm, dry weather, the tools, materials, and people.

The material is supplied in either fifty-gallon drums or five-gallon cans. It is slightly more expensive in the cans, but you'll have to spend the extra money, since the drums are virtually impossible to move except with heavy equipment.

Once you have emptied the first can, you will have more room for mixing, using your empties to pour into. For the first can or two, use the pail that I listed among the tools. Pour off enough material to leave room for a little water.

Follow the directions carefully in regard to dilution. Too much water will destroy the effectiveness of the emulsion. The emulsion should be thick enough so that it is not runny; when poured out onto the court, it should not spread very much. On the other hand, it should not be too stiff to spread evenly and smoothly with the squeegees.

Pouring

When you have thoroughly mixed the first pail, pour a thick stream of it along one edge or one end of the court. The stream should be about four or five inches wide and should lie about a foot from the edge of the court, so that when the squeegee is pulled along the edge, the emulsion spreads out to cover the edge evenly.

Working the Squeegees

To cover the edge of the court evenly with the first row of emulsion, angle the squeegee slightly (about 45 degrees) toward the edge. On all successive rows, until the very last one, angle the squeegees (about 45 degrees) away from the finished rows, so that no material is left to make a ridge (see Figure 69).

There should always be enough emulsion poured for the squeegee so that some of the emulsion will slide off the trailing edge of the squeegee and leave a row of unspread emulsion behind. This unspread emulsion is called the *windrow*. More emulsion should then be added to this windrow (poured from the can) so there is enough for the squeegee to spread, again leaving a continuous windrow. The 45-degree angle of the squeegees should spread the material smoothly and prevent any material from overflowing the *leading* edge.

The mixing and pouring should keep easy pace with the spread-

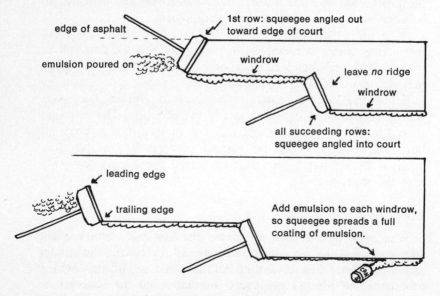

FIGURE 69. Applying the asphaltic emulsion

ing process, to cover the whole court with an even layer of emulsion. If there are any accidental ridges left, don't try to go back and fix them. Wait until the court is dry enough to walk on and then scrape them away with a trowel or putty knife.

Change Directions

It might help to even out any slight imperfections if you apply the second layer at right angles to the first and continue changing directions until you have applied all the material required to meet the manufacturer's specifications for the amount of emulsion per square foot. If you applied the first layer going from one side to the other, apply the second layer going from end to end.

The Effect of Temperature

On a moderately warm day in the sixties or low seventies, the emulsion should spread a little more thickly. If the temperature gets very high—in the high eighties or nineties—the material may dry too quickly; you will have to spray the court with water to cool and dampen it ahead of the work. Also, the individual layers may be thinner because of the heat. This will mean more work because it will take more layers to put down the specified amount of emulsion.

One More Level Check

When you have finished applying the asphaltic emulsion and it is thoroughly dry, you have one more chance to get rid of birdbaths. Flood the court once more, let it drain, and again use the keel to mark the outline of puddles that are deeper than $\frac{1}{16}$ inch.

Using the same straightedge method, aided by your squeegees, fill in the depressions with asphaltic emulsion. Let it dry thoroughly, and then you will be ready for the color coat.

Applying the Color Coat

The color coat is applied in exactly the same manner as the asphaltic-emulsion playing surface. Again, spread the quantity of color coat per square foot that the manufacturer specifies. When it dries, you will be ready to reline the court as described in Chapter 11.

13.

Maintenance and Repair

When it comes to maintenance, nonporous and porous courts have nothing in common beyond their function: to provide the best possible area for tennis.

Nonporous Courts

Maintenance

Keep your nonporous court free of dirt and vegetable matter. Sweep off leaves, sticks, earth, pebbles, and any other material that is blown, washed, thrown, or kicked onto the court.

A push broom with moderately heavy bristles will do this job quite well, and it will also push off and/or spread small puddles left from a rain, so that they will dry quickly. You will find that fine particles of earth will tend to settle in puddle areas and gradually discolor the paint. You can help prevent this situation by scrubbing the puddle areas two or three times a season with a brush and a hose. If they get badly stained, use a *little* mild detergent—but be sure to rinse it all off with the hose.

If you have edged the court with lawn grass, be sure that the earth and grass do not creep onto the asphaltic-emulsion surface and cause it to deteriorate. With an edger or a spade, trim the earth and grass just clear of the court material.

Do not attempt to remove snow and ice from the court by scraping or shoveling. You may damage the playing surface. Just wait for a thaw.

Repair

Patching

The surface may need some repair after five or six years of weathering and use.

Even the best-built court in the world may settle slightly over the years, resulting in a small increase in the depth of some bird-baths. The cure for this will be to repeat the patching process with the asphaltic emulsion, then repaint court and lines.

If the puddling has not changed noticeably but the paint has weathered, simply repaint the court and lines. It is a good idea to repaint every five or six years, to protect the asphaltic emulsion and the asphalt itself.

If cracks have developed, find out what caused them. Is there a tree near enough to the court to be sending a root under the surface? If so, you may have to remove the tree and also dig down next to the court to cut the root off. If the root has made a ridge, along with the crack, you can try to level the raised area with a sledge hammer. Then apply asphaltic emulsion into and over the crack and repaint as needed to cover. If the ridge and crack are too large to cure with these simple methods, you may have to dig up the asphalt and go down to the subbase to discover the problem. If the cause is a growing root, dig it out and replace all layers. Cold asphalt patch can be bought at a building supply store. If the cause appears to be heaving from water that has frozen before draining away (this would not happen if the drainage had been properly planned during construction), you may be able to solve the problem by digging out more of the subbase and increasing the depth of the crushed rock in that area. You will then have to patch in layers of asphalt, reapply playing surface material, and repaint. Be sure that each level is compacted thoroughly as you fill in.

General Heaving

If a nonporous court heaves and breaks up in many spots over the area of the court, there is no easy cure, for this means that the drainage is entirely inadequate. There are two possible cures: you can apply a whole new asphalt base on top of the old one, thereby achieving a smooth court again, or you can break up the whole court, remove the asphalt and start the whole job over with properly installed drainage. The latter course is extremely difficult and expensive. Breaking up and removing six inches of asphalt takes heavy equipment and manpower, both of which will be expensive. If the general heaving did not take place for ten or more years, it is probably worth gambling on the first option. It would also be wise to increase the drainage ditches around the court area, in order to lessen the amount of water that can run under the court. Better drainage, plus the additional weight of the new asphalt layer, will tend to avert a recurrence of the problem.

Sealing the Cracks

If you live in an area where there is frost, it is essential that you seal any cracks in the court surface before each winter. If water is allowed to get into the cracks and freeze, the problem will become more serious.

Porous Courts

Maintenance

Rolling

The porous court should be rolled every day for the first week or ten days after completion. This rolling should be done in both directions: cross-court and then lengthwise. The court must be damp enough so that the greenstone will pack under the weight of the roller. When the crushed greenstone surface turns gray, it needs moisture.

After the first ten days, follow the routine presented in the simple table on page 158. Unless you put in a sprinkler system, you will have to spend a great many hours every week with a hose in your hand, wetting the court down.

You must own either a hand roller or motor roller which should weigh 500 pounds for the best results. You need not roll in both directions every time for weekly maintenance, but it is a good idea to alternate the direction of rolling. It will help to even the material and the compaction.

Be sure the lines are kept down flat so that the brushing doesn't sweep grit under them and build them up. Once that happens, the problem will get worse and worse.

Treating the Fast-dry Material

Calcium chloride is used to treat the fast-dry material because it increases water retention and when damp, helps to bind the particles of the court surface. When the fast-dry material is shipped to you, it will probably have been treated with calcium chloride. If not, you will have to treat the material yourself.

You should reapply calcium chloride to the whole court area twice each season: in the spring and again in July or August, when the court begins to dry too quickly for easy maintenance. In an extraordinarily dry climate, you may have to make three or more applications.

At the end of the day, when the sun will no longer have a drying effect, sprinkle three hundred to four hundred pounds of the chemical over the whole court. Brush off any that gets onto the lines, which it will tend to rot. If there is enough water in the atmosphere, the calcium chloride will have dissolved by morning. You should then brush and roll the court. If there is any evidence that the calcium chloride has not all dissolved, water the court and after the water has soaked in thoroughly, brush and roll.

The Line Tapes

The line tapes should be painted each spring with a good water resistant paint.

Off-Season Maintenance

Porous courts must be protected from the effects of extreme winter weather. If you live where the ground freezes hard for weeks at a time, it is advisable to cover your court with plastic or water resistant paper—a paper treated with tar, for instance—during the cold months. It would be best not to use tar paper, which will expose the surface directly to the tar. A paper impregnated with tar or asphalt is preferable.

Put down the paper or plastic sheets on the downhill side of the court first and overlap each section so the water will run off the court. Then cover the paper or plastic with two or three inches of straw—or even more in the extreme deep-freeze areas of the country—and then use some chicken wire to hold the straw in place.

This winter blanket will protect the surface from precipitation and from most of the heaving effect of the frost. Covering the court requires a lot of work, but if you don't do it, you will be very unhappy in the spring if you find the base thrust up through the fast-dry material over large areas of the court. The consequent repair job will require far more work than the blanket and will never bring the court back to its original condition.

If you live in Florida or Southern California or any other semitropical region, you can play all year on a porous court with the same maintenance schedule outlined earlier.

MAINTENANCE SCHEDULE

	ROLLING	WATERING	BRUSHING
First 7 to 10 days (new court)	Once a day, two directions, for first 7 to 10 days	Every day before rolling, unless court is thoroughly damp from rain	Every day before rolling and at end of play
Regularly through playing season	Once a week and after any substantial rainfall, alternating directions	Enough to keep court damp. When greenstone begins to look gray, it's dry: time to water	After every day's play, after every watering, before every rolling

Repair

Patching

If any hollows or depressions appear in the surface, fill them with the crushed greenstone material, tamp it down and water it. Roll the area, and if it appears even with the rest of the court, you are finished. If it is still slightly hollow, repeat the process; if it is high, work a little of it off with a straightedge and roll again.

If any of the base material works up through the surface in the spring, remove it and following the patching instructions, fill any hollows.

Manufacturers and Suppliers

It would not be possible to give you the names and addresses of every manufacturer of tennis-related products that you may want— or even a tenth of these companies. What follows is a small sample, along with sources of further information.

Associations

UNITED STATES TENNIS ASSOCIATION (USTA)
51 East 42 Street
New York, N.Y. 10017

The association sells a booklet titled *Tennis Courts,* which covers construction, maintenance, and equipment. It contains a great deal of useful information, although it does not tell you how to build a tennis court yourself.

The association can also be useful in answering specific questions you may have about any aspect of the court or the game. It can supply you with tennis rule books, films, publications, and other information. You can write to the USTA Education and Research Committee, 71 University Place, Princeton, N.J. 08540, for more information.

U.S. TENNIS COURT AND TRACK BUILDERS ASSOCIATION
1201 Waukegan Road
Glenview, Ill. 60025

In addition to supplying you with names and addresses of all its members, this group issues specifications for construction and maintenance of a variety of courts. These are specifications, not instructions. They set standards for all courts and tracks installed by association members, so that the public can have confidence in any contract or product of a member company.

Manufacturers of Asphaltic-Emulsion Tennis Court Surfaces

CHEVRON ASPHALT COMPANY
San Francisco, Calif. 94119
Perth Amboy, N.J. 08862
Baltimore, Md. 21203
Cincinnati, Ohio, 45238
Tucson, Ariz. 85703

Chevron has other offices, perhaps nearer to you than any of these, and if you write, the company will give you that information, as well as the address of the nearest plant from which you can obtain the materials.

Laykold, Grasstex surfaces

Laykold is by far the easier of the two to apply, and it is what we used for our court. Grasstex is a cushioned surface and is not only a little more comfortable for your feet but more expensive. Ask the company to send you specifications for all its surfacing products and study them carefully. If you have specific questions about how to work with the materials, Chevron will be helpful in answering them. You may also get some help by showing the specifications to your asphalt man and discussing application techniques with him.

RECREATION TECHNOLOGY COMPANY
P.O. Box 408
Wooster, Ohio 44691
Rech-Tech Surfacer. Write for specifications.

COSMICOAT INC.
3400 Cleveland Road
P.O. Box 73
Wooster, Ohio 44691
Cosmicolor Tennis Court Surfacing Products: Tenibase, Tenicoat, Teniline.

FLINTKOTE INDUSTRIAL PRODUCTS
480 Central Avenue
East Rutherford, N.J. 07073
Decoralt color systems: Decobase, Decoturf

TRUFLEX RECREATIONAL COATINGS
1760 Rever Beach Parkway
Everett, Mass. 02149
TruFlex 3-Coat System, TruFlex Cushion System

TENNIS COURT CONSTRUCTORS
1455 New York Avenue
Huntington Station, N.Y. 11746
Velvetop Acrylic Filler (resurfacer), Velvetop Wearever

CALIFORNIA PRODUCTS CORP.
P.O. Box 30
169 Waverly Street
Cambridge, Mass. 02139
Plexipave, Plexicushion

Manufacturers of Porous-Court Material

HAR-TRU® CORPORATION
Box 569
Hagerstown, Md. 21740
Har-Tru® (crushed crystalline greenstone)

Har-Tru® is now available in most parts of the country. Write to Mr. R. M. Helm at Har-Tru, and he will be glad to supply you with information about obtaining the material and also applying it.

Estimating Costs

Nonporous Court

Item	Our cost (1971)	Estimate: your cost	Actual cost
Transit rental	$ 60.00		
Tools	46.00		
Weedkiller	8.00		
Wood for stakes, mason's cord	6.00		
Bulldozer, bucket loader, ditch-digger	200.00		
Drainpipe	45.00		
Stone for fill	63.00		
Motor roller, rental	70.00		
1½-inch stone	592.00		
⅝-inch stone	333.00		
Screenings	182.00		
Cement	56.00		

Item	Our cost (1971)	Estimate: your cost	Actual cost
Sand	34.00		
Wood, for net-post plugs	12.00		
Asphalt	3850.00		
Net posts and net	145.00		
Bulldozer, backhoe, truck (grading)	114.00		
Fencing	1200.00		
Grass seed	26.00		
Motor roller, rental (landscaping)	35.00		
Nylon netting (one side of court)	85.00		
Line paint, acrylic latex	10.00		
Asphaltic emulsion	700.00		
Other items			
	$7872.00		

Porous Court

Item	Cost (1971)	Estimate: your cost	Actual cost
Transit rental	$ 60.00		
Tools	46.00		
Weedkiller	8.00		
Wood for stakes, mason's cord	6.00		
Bulldozer, bucket loader, ditch-digger	300.00		
Drainpipe	150.00		
Stone for fill	75.00		
Motor roller, rental	70.00		
¾-inch stone	450.00		
Screenings	185.00		
Cement	56.00		
Sand	34.00		
Wood, for net-post plugs	12.00		
Fast-dry material (f.o.b. New City, N.Y.)	1750.00		

Item	Cost (1971)	Estimate: your cost	Actual cost
Net posts and net	145.00		
Bulldozer, backhoe, truck (grading)	114.00		
Fencing	1200.00		
Grass seed	26.00		
Motor roller, rental (landscaping)	35.00		
Nylon netting (one side of court)	85.00		
Hand roller (purchase)	100.00		
Fabric liner and nails	110.00		
Other items			

$5017.00

Playing Qualities of Various Surfaces

		Cement	Non-cushioned asphalt[1]	Cushioned asphalt[2]	Plastic and rubber[3]	Crushed stone	Clay	Grass
RESILIENCE[4]	Low	X	X					
	Medium		X	X				
	High			X	X	X	X	X
TRACTION[5]	Low					X	X	X
	Medium							
	High	X	X	X	X[6]			
BOUNCE	Low					X	X	X
	Medium			X	X	X	X	
	High	X	X	X				

[1] *Noncushioned asphalt:* it is assumed that a playing surface has been applied to the asphalt. Plain asphalt is not a very pleasant surface to play on. The surfaces that are available contain enough fiber materials to make them smoother and softer than asphalt.

[2] *Cushioned asphalt:* usually this means a cushioning layer is applied between the asphalt and the playing surface, giving the court extra resilience. It is therefore somewhat easier on the feet and legs.

[3] *Plastic and rubber:* there are various surface compounds that have appeared in recent years, and every year will probably see new ones. They must be applied by their manufacturers or with special machinery in most cases because they are either applied hot or molten with chemical solvents and are not within the scope of amateur workers.

[4] *Resilience:* this is the "give," or relative softness or hardness of the surface under the weight of the foot.

[5] *Traction:* this refers to the "grip," that your sneakers have on the surface.

[6] Many of the plastic or rubberized surfaces do not allow any sliding of the sneaker and may be dangerous if you aren't used to them. You can easily twist an ankle if you are used to sliding.

Calculating Quantities

Converting Measurements

METRIC EQUIVALENTS

U.S. Units	*U.S. Equivalents*	*Metric equivalents*
inch	.083 foot	2.54 centimeters
foot	12 inches	.3048 meters
yard	36 inches, 3 feet	.9144 meters
square inch	.007 square foot	6.4516 square centimeters
square foot	144 square inches	929.030 square centimeters
square yard	1,296 square inches	.836 square meter
acre	43,560 square feet	4,047 square meters
square mile	640 acres	2,590 square kilometers
cubic inch	.00058 cubic foot	16.387 cubic centimeters
cubic foot	1,728 cubic inches	.028 cubic meter
cubic yard	27 cubic feet	.765 cubic meter
quart	57.75 cubic inches	.946 liter
gallon	231 cubic inches, 4 quarts	3.785 liters
pound	16 ounces	453.59237 grams
ton	2,000 pounds	.907 metric ton, 907 kilograms

You know	*Multiply by*	*To convert to*
inches	2.54	centimeters
feet	30.48	centimeters
yards	.91	meters
miles	1.61	kilometers

OR

millimeters	.04	inches
centimeters	.39	inches
meters	3.28	feet
meters	1.09	yards
kilometers	.62	miles

You know	*Multiply by*	*To convert to*
quarts	.95	liters
gallons	3.78	liters
cubic inches	16.39	cubic centimeters
cubic feet	.03	cubic meters
cubic yards	.76	cubic meters

OR

liters	.26	gallons
cubic centimeters	.061	cubic inches
cubic meters	35.32	cubic feet
cubic meters	1.31	cubic yards

TEMPERATURES

You know	*Multiply by*	*To convert to*
Fahrenheit temperature	$\frac{5}{9}$, *after* subtracting 32	Celsius temperature
Celsius temperature	$\frac{9}{5}$, then add 32	Fahrenheit temperature

Calculating Quantities of Material

To calculate the quantities of material you will need for the net-post holes, you can use the following simple formula for finding the volume of a cylindrical shape. Volume is equivalent to pi times the radius squared times the height ($\pi r^2 h = V$)

Using my recommendations, this is:
$3.1416 \times 30 \times 30 \times 36 = 101,787.84$ cubic inches
Divide this by 1,728 to get 58.905 cubic feet.
Concrete weighs approximately 145 pounds per cubic foot.
Stone weighs a little more, from 150 to 160 pounds per cubic foot.
Sand weighs between 90 and 120 pounds per cubic foot.

To calculate quantities of material per inch of depth for a 7,200 square-foot court (120 by 60 feet), each inch of depth is 22.22222 cubic yards. Thus, 4 inches of depth is 88.88888 cubic yards of material.

Scheduling Your Time

Job Phase	Working Days (Estimate)	Required Weather
PHASE ONE		
Pick site and position of court	Flexible	Any
Lay out schedule with help of these pages	Flexible	Any
Talk to people about helping you	Flexible	Any
Accumulate necessary tools	Flexible	Any
Find bulldozer man	Flexible	Any
Inquire about other outside help with rock base, asphalt, fast-dry material	Flexible	Any
Budget	Flexible	Any
Learn to use transit; study Chapter 4; field practice	2	No precipitation for field practice

Job Phase	Working Days (Estimate)	Required Weather
PHASE TWO		
Cut trees, remove stumps, grade with bulldozer. Remove all large rocks, all vegetable matter	2–5	Above freezing. Ground not frozen
Grade to 2-inch tolerance with transit	1	No precipitation
Dig drainage ditches, install drainpipe, put in stone, fill	2–5	Light precipitation not a problem
Recheck entire grid with transit, compact with 1,000-lb. roller	1	Light precipitation okay
PHASE THREE *(nonporous courts)*		
Lay 1½-inch crushed rock (highway ballast)	2–3	Earth firm and dry enough to support heavy truck
Level rock with bulldozer, hand rakes, and transit	2–3	Earth firm and dry
Compact stone with 1,000-lb. motor roller. Check grid with transit	1	Earth firm and dry
Lay ⅝-inch or ¾-inch crushed stone compensating for errors in 1½-inch stone layer	2	Earth firm enough to support heavy truck
Level stone with hand rakes and transit	2	Dry weather (for the transit)
Compact stone with 1,000-lb. roller, check grid with transit	1	Dry weather
Lay screenings	1	Light rain is okay
Level screenings with hand rakes, to ¼ inch of desired plane	1	Dry weather

Job Phase	*Working Days (Estimate)*	*Required Weather*
Compact screenings with 1,000-lb. roller, check with transit and make corrections to within ¼ inch of desired plane	1	Dry weather Note: moderate rain between stages of work in phase 3 okay

PHASE FOUR

(nonporous courts)

Build net-post plugs (can be done during phase 3)	2	Indoor work
Measure for position of net-post plugs and put them in place	½	Damp okay
Measure for and install stakes and strings to guide asphalt laying	½	Damp okay
Lay first layer of asphalt	2–3	Light rain okay but annoying
Roll asphalt	½	Light rain okay but annoying
Check with transit and paint grid readings on asphalt	½	Dry
Patch if needed to bring within ¼ inch of desired plane, checking work with transit	½	Dry
Lay top layer of asphalt	2	Light rain okay but annoying
Roll asphalt	½	Light rain okay but annoying
Check with transit and by flooding with water	½	Dry
Patch if needed to bring within ¼ inch of desired plane, checking work with transit	½	Dry

Job Phase	Working Days (Estimate)	Required Weather
Let asphalt cure Note: phase 5 can be completed during curing of asphalt	21–42	Any

PHASES THREE AND FOUR
(porous courts only)

Job Phase	Working Days (Estimate)	Required Weather
Dig sprinkler system trenches and drain pit	2	Any
Lay brick curb	3	Dry
Prepare stakes and vertical screed strips for crushed stone, horizontal screed strips for fast-dry material and prepare straightedge	2	Can be done indoors
Using transit, install stakes and screed strips for ¾-inch crushed stone	1–2	Dry
Lay, level, and compact ¾-inch stone	2–3	Dry
Spread, level, and compact screenings	1–2	Dry
Remove screed strips and stakes and fill and compact crevices	1	Damp okay
Roll court with 1,000-lb. roller	½	Damp okay
Lay screed strips and fast-dry material, one row at a time	6	Dry
Compact court with 500–600-lb. roller	½	Damp okay
Install sprinkler heads	1	Damp okay

PHASE FIVE

Job Phase	Working Days (Estimate)	Required Weather
Dig net-post holes	2	Any
Install net posts	2	Damp okay
Dig fence-post holes	1 man-hour per hole	Rain okay but annoying

Job Phase	Working Days (Estimate)	Required Weather
Install fence posts	1 man-hour per hole	Dry
Put up fencing	Depends on kind and amount	Dry
Landscape (fill, shape, rake, seed, roll, water)	Depends on extent of job	Damp okay
Line court (optional for non-porous court depending on desire to play during asphalt curing)	1–2	Dry
PHASE SIX *(nonporous courts only) (After asphalt has cured)*		
Outline puddle areas after rain or after flooding	½	Dry
Patch puddle areas using straightedge	1	Dry
Squeegee on asphaltic-emulsion playing surface	1	Dry
Squeegee on tennis court color coat	½	Dry
Line (or reline) court	½	Dry

Accessories

PUSH BROOM. Useful for sweeping things off the nonporous court. Also good for spreading out small puddles so they will dry up quickly (though more efficient puddle work is done with the Rol-Dri).

ROL-DRI. A rolling sponge with a long handle. It pushes the water off the court in a thirty-inch swath. The rolling squeegee sponge is replaceable when it wears out. *Nothing* else does as well for removing water from a court. It also helps dry the grass around the court. If you have used the grass-strip ·alternative (see Chapter 6), you will find this very handy. (Rol-Dri, Inc., 7731 Long Point Road, Suite 4, Houston, Tex. 77002)

BALL-RETRIEVER. A wire basket with a handle that makes it easy to pick up dozens of balls when you are practicing or teaching. There are several makes and designs, which you will find advertised in tennis publications.

BALL MACHINE. This machine is good for practicing specific shots, hit over and over to the same place. It's hard to find friends who are willing and able to do this for you. The prices start in the $300 range and go on up. But a small machine is quite adequate for private use.

REBOUND NET. Some prefer this to a wooden practice backboard. Some rebound nets can be adjusted to throw the balls back at different angles and different speeds.

DRAG BRUSH. For smoothing out the crushed greenstone of the porous court. A necessity.

LINE-SWEEPER. Also a necessity for the porous court, to clean the lines after using the drag brush.

ROLLER. A motorized 500-to-600-pound roller is a good investment for the porous court. If you do not want to spend the money, you will need to buy one that you pull and push by hand. Whether motorized or manual, this, too, is a necessity for the porous court.

TABLE. Have at least one weather-proof table beside the court, for ball cans, drinks, glasses, and other comforts.

CHAIRS. For those who watch or wait—and for those who play. If the top players in the world sit down for a rest when they change courts, why shouldn't we, who may be less fit? It's better to be remembered for how well you played than for your endurance.

WATER THERMOS OR PITCHER. Water loss is exhausting. On a very hot day have a little before you play and a sip or two every once in a while during the game.

INDEX